DEPRESSION
A Stubborn Darkness

LIGHT FOR THE PATH

﷽VantagePoint

A series published in cooperation with
THE CHRISTIAN COUNSELING AND EDUCATIONAL
FOUNDATION
Glenside, Pennsylvania

Susan Lutz, Series Editor

Other books by our authors:

Edward T. Welch, *When People Are Big and God Is Small:
Overcoming Peer Pressure, Codependency, and the Fear of Man*
Paul David Tripp, *Age of Opportunity: A Biblical Guide to
Parenting Teens*
Edward T. Welch, *Blame It on the Brain? Distinguishing Chemical
Imbalances, Brain Disorders, and Disobedience*
James C. Petty, *Step by Step: Divine Guidance for Ordinary
Christians*
Paul David Tripp, *War of Words: Getting to the Heart of Your
Communication Struggles*
Edward T. Welch, *Addictions – A Banquet in the Grave: Finding
Hope in the Power of the Gospel*
Paul David Tripp, *Instruments in the Redeemer's Hands: People in
Need of Change Helping People in Need of Change*
David Powlison, *Seeing with New Eyes: Counseling and the Human
Condition through the Lens of Scripture*

DEPRESSION
A STUBBORN DARKNESS

LIGHT FOR THE PATH

EDWARD T. WELCH

3143 S. STRATFORD ROAD, WINSTON-SALEM, NC 27103-5825
WWW.PUNCHBOOKSTORE.COM

Scripture quotations are from the HOLY BIBLE, NEW INTERNATIONAL VERSION®. NIV®. Copyright © 1973, 1978, 1984 by International Bible Society. Used by permission of Zondervan Publishing House. All rights reserved.

Italics in Scripture quotations indicate emphasis added.

Cover design and photograph by Andy Robbins

ISBN: 0-9762308-0-1

Printed in the United States of America

To my father
W. Edward Welch,

who, on this side of heaven,
after years of depression, guilt, and worry,
persisted on an ordinary yet heroic path
with quiet wisdom
and is finding joy

Contents

Contents

Acknowledgments

If this book has been able to capture the experience of depression, it is because men and women, especially those who came for counseling to The Christian Counseling and Educational Foundation (CCEF), were willing to tell me their stories, even when I was slow to understand. My students from Westminster Theological Seminary and CCEF filled in the rest.

The actual writing was done because of the generous sabbatical policy given by CCEF. As such, I am indebted to the CCEF board, faculty, administrative staff, and contributors. The faculty and administrative staff picked up tasks I dropped and generally covered for me in such a way that I still had a job when I returned. Sue Lutz once again provided keen editorial direction, as she has on almost every book I have completed. She is certainly not allowed to retire before I do.

My wife and daughters are now accustomed to times when I am preoccupied with a manuscript, and they take it in stride. But I will never take their love, understanding and encouragement for granted.

Introduction

CHAPTER 1

The Path Ahead

In the middle of the journey of our life
I found myself in a dark wood,
For I had lost the right path.
                                        Dante

When you are depressed, how can you take a step, let alone a journey?

When all vital energy is devoted to staying alive and just making it to the next hour, how can you add anything else – like hope – to your day?

These are the "how to" questions that, in the face of depression, seem almost impossible to answer. Pages of homework and practical suggestions could, indeed, fill many books, but they are unlikely to make you feel alive.

What you need must go deeper than practical advice. You don't need a series of "how tos." In fact, you could probably write a credible list of "how tos" yourself. You already know many things you *could* do and you have probably done some of them.

Chapter One

Depression, and the host of feelings and thoughts that get crammed into the word, plead for a "why." First, why is this happening to me? Then, why love? Why work? Why worship? Why believe? Why live? Why bother? The depressive heart resonates more with "Vanity of vanity, all is vanity" than with "101 steps to combat depression." A list of "how tos" can't speak to issues of purpose, hope, and the fundamental questions of existence and belief that depression inevitably raises. It's not surprising that while Prozac is being heralded as the cure, philosophers are also finding a niche in helping those who are depressed.

So, on the path ahead, look for a partnership between whys and how tos. When the why questions appear, they will be religious – as all why questions are. They will be about God. Depression, of course, does that – it takes you back to the basic questions of life. Ignore them to focus on the how questions and you might find a temporary shortcut to mental relief, but your heart will still be famished.

The Basic Idea

Depression is a form of suffering that can't be reduced to one universal cause. This means that family and friends can't rush in armed with THE answer. Instead, they must be willing to postpone swearing allegiance to a particular theory, and take time to know the depressed person and work together with him or her. What we do know is that depression is painful and, if you have never experienced it, hard to understand. Like most forms of suffering, it feels private and isolating.

We also know that those who feel overwhelmed by depression share in a fundamental humanness. You will find in them the struggles and maladies that are common to us all.

Don't let the technical, scientific diagnosis keep you from seeing these ordinary problems. Instead, when in doubt, expect to find ordinary humanness just below the surface, in the form of fear, anger, guilt, shame, jealousy, wants, despair over loss, physical weaknesses and other problems that are present in every person. Depression is not always caused by these things, but it is always an occasion to consider them.

Are There "Right" Emotions?

It is common for spiritually mature men and women who feel depressed to think that they are doing something wrong. After all, Scripture is filled with words of joy and happy hearts. When they aren't feeling happy, they feel that they must be missing something or that God is punishing them until they learn some hidden lesson.

On earth, however, God doesn't prescribe a happy life. He doesn't legislate emotions. Look at some of the Psalms. They are written by people of great faith, yet they run the emotional gamut. One even ends with "darkness is my closest friend" (Ps. 88:18). When your emotions feel muted or always low, when you are unable to experience the highs and lows you once did, the important question is, "Where do you turn – or, to whom do you turn – when you are depressed?"

A Way to Proceed

If you are depressed, the chapters that follow are intended to be brief and, at times, provocative. If you want to help someone who is depressed, the chapters are intended to give you direction and to be used as actual readings you can share with the depressed person. My hope is that the book will encourage partnerships between depressed people and those who love them. Suffering is not a journey we should take alone. There are too many places where we are tempted to give up and too many times we can't see clearly. So if you are depressed, read this book with a wise friend. If you want to help, ask the depressed person to read it with you, or select particular chapters to read together.

The Journey of a Pilgrim

You will encounter a number of images in the coming chapters, such as darkness or light, numbness or vitality, and surrender or waging battle. Most prominent will be the journey of a pilgrim. Whether we sense it or not, we are walking a path that always confronts us with a choice. Each day we stand at a crossroads and make decisions of significant consequence.

The idea of heading out on a trek is not a pleasing thought when you are depressed, but at least you are in good company, which should offer some comfort. Beginning with Abraham, God has called people to leave a familiar place, set out in a new direction, put the past behind, face unknown hazards, get to a point of desperation, call out for help, and look forward to something (or someone) better.

Origen, an old saint of the church, offered this encouragement.

> "My soul has long been on pilgrimage" (Ps. 119:54). Understand, then, if you can, what the pilgrimages of the soul are, especially when it laments with groaning and grief that it has been on pilgrimage so long. We understand these pilgrimages only dully and darkly so long as the pilgrimage still lasts. But when the soul has returned to its rest, that is, to the homeland of paradise, it will be taught more truly and will

understand more truly the meaning of what the pilgrimage was.[1]

He is right. On this side of heaven we walk by faith and don't have all the answers we would like. But there is reason to believe that you will find certain hopes fulfilled even on this side of paradise.

---

[1] Origen, Homily XXVII On Numbers, sec. 4, CWS, 250. Cited in Thomas Oden, *Classical Pastoral Care, Vol.4 Crisis Ministries* (Grand Rapids: Baker, 1994) p.6.

CHAPTER 2

How Depression Feels

"Hell" comes up often. "Hell came to pay me a surprise visit."
"If there is a hell upon earth, it is to be found in a melancholy
heart," observed Robert Burton in the 1600s. The poet Robert
Lowell wrote, "I myself am hell." A mother describes her child's
experience as "Danny's Descent into Hell." "A Room in Hell."
"A lonely, private hell." John of the Cross called it "the dark
night of the soul." "Hellish torments," recounted J. B. Phillips.
"Hell's black depths," said William Styron, author of *Sophie's
Choice* and other popular but sometimes dark novels.[1] As Dante
understood, there is an intimate connection between hell and the
hopelessness of depression. The entrance to Dante's version of
hell read, "Abandon all hope, ye who enter here."

---

[1] Quotes in this paragraph are from the following sources: Andrew Solomon, "Anatomy of
Melancholy," *The New Yorker*, January 12, 1998, p. 61. Robert Burton cited in John Green and
James Jefferson, *Depression and Its Treatment* (New York: Warner, 1992), p. 4. Robert Lowell,
"Skunk Hour." Sandra McCoy, "Danny's Descent into Hell," A *Reader's Digest Reprint.* Martha
Manning, *Undercurrents: A Therapist's Reckoning with Depression* (New York: Harper, 1995), p. 10.
Lillian V. Grissen, *A Path Through the Sea* (Grand Rapids: Eerdmans, 1993), p. 9. J. B. Phillips,
The Price of Success (New York: Shaw, 1985), p. 201. William Styron, *Darkness Visible* (New York:
Vintage, 1990), p. 84. Unattributed quotes throughout this chapter are from conversations with
individuals.

Chapter Two

Depressive speech is poetic. Prose does not capture the experience, so it is either poetry or silence. Depressed people are eloquent, even when they feel empty at their emotional core, devoid of personhood.

> When the doctor came to my room, he said, "I am going to ask you a question. If you don't feel ready to answer it, please don't." Then he asked, "Who are you?"
> I panicked. "What do you mean?"
> "When you look inside, who do you see?"
> It was horrible. When I looked inside I couldn't see anyone. All I saw was a black hole.
> "'I am no one," I said.

The images are dark and evocative. Desperately alone, doom, black holes, deep wells, emptiness. "I felt like I was walking through a field of dead flowers and found one beautiful rose, but when I bent down to smell it I fell into an invisible hole." "I heard my silent scream echo through and pierce my empty soul." "There is nothing I hate more than nothing."[2] "My heart is empty. All the fountains that should run with longing, are in me dried up."[3] "It is entirely natural to think ceaselessly of oblivion." "I feel as though I died a few weeks ago and my body hasn't found out yet."

> Depression . . . involves a complete absence: absence of affect, absence of feeling, absence of response,

---

[2] Edie Bricknell, "Nothing."

[3] C. S. Lewis, "The Naked Seed." *Poems by C. S. Lewis* (Grand Rapids: Eerdmans, 1964), p.117.

[4] Andrew Solomon, "Anatomy of Melancholy," *The New Yorker*, January 12, 1998, p.53.

absence of interest. The pain you feel in the course of a major clinical depression is an attempt on nature's part . . . to fill up the empty space. But for all intents and purposes, the deeply depressed are just the walking, waking dead.[5]

The mental pain seems unbearable. Time stands still. "I can't go on," said a twelve-year-old girl. "I could weep by the hour like a child, and yet I knew not what I wept for," recounted Spurgeon of one of his many episodes.[6] "A veritable howling tempest in the brain."[7] "Malignant sadness."[8] "My bones wasted away through my groaning all day long."[9] "The unhappiness was like dust that infiltrated everything." "I am now a man of despair, rejected, abandoned, shut up in this iron cage from which there is no escape."[10] "The iron bolt ... mysteriously fastens the door of hope and holds our spirits in gloomy prison."[11]

> Profound melancholia is a day-in day-out, night-in night-out, almost arterial level of agony. It is a pitiless, unrelenting pain that affords no window of hope, no alternative to a grim and brackish existence, and no respite from the cold undercurrents of

---

[5] Elizabeth Wurtzel, *Prozac Nation* (New York: Riverhead), p. 22.

[6] Darrel Amundsen, "The Anguish and Agonies of Charles Spurgeon," *Christian History*, 10 (1991), p. 64.

[7] Styron, p. 38.

[8] "Spirit of the Age," *The Economist*, December 19, 1998, p. 113.

[9] Psalm 32:3.

[10] J. Bunyan, *Pilgrim's Progress* (Chicago: Moody, 1964), p. 33.

[11] Charles Spurgeon, *Lectures to My Students* (Grand Rapids: Zondervan, 1972), p. 24.

thought and feeling that dominate the horribly restless nights of despair.[12]

But it is not just pain. It feels like meaningless pain. "That is all I want in life: for this pain to seem purposeful."[13] If pain leads to childbirth, it is tolerable, but if it just leads to blackness or nothing, then it threatens to destroy.

Abraham Lincoln thought the pain would lead to death; the body couldn't tolerate it.

> I am now the most miserable man living. If what I feel were equally distributed to the whole human family, there would not be one cheerful face on earth. Whether I shall ever be better, I cannot tell; I awfully forbode I shall not. To remain as I am is impossible. I must die or be better, it appears to me.[14]

What tortures many people is the fact that they *don't* die. "Exhaustion combined with sleeplessness is a rare torture." "The pain seeps into everything." The thought that they might remain in this horrible state is too much to consider. "No one knows how badly I want to die." But death has its own horrors. It feels like a vanishing point where they cease to exist at all. And what about the uncertainty of life after death? Is there annihilation? Will divine judgment crush and destroy? You are without peer in fearing the worst.

"There was no control on my mind – thoughts ravaged me,

---

[12] Jamison, *An Unquiet Mind* (New York: Random House, 1995), p. 114.

[13] Wurtzel, p. 50.

[14] Cited in John H. Greist and James W. Jefferson, *Depression and Its Treatment* (New York: Warner, 1992), p. 8.

brutally harsh ideas, thoroughly crushed ideals, incomprehensible feelings." The mind is stuck. How can people think about anything else when *it* is there? "I'm in a straitjacket." "I'm completely bound and tied up – there is a gag in my mouth." Without one's normal mental resources, the world is frightening. Panic. Left unchecked, hallucinations and delusions can seize the imagination with such force that they are indistinguishable from reality itself. Self-reliance seems impossible. Infantile dependence is the only way to survive. Being alone is terrifying. Abandonment is a constant fear. "I fear everyone and everything."

> I tried to sleep but couldn't. Part of it was that I was scared to wake up with a feeling of panic in the pit of my stomach. Anxiety was always present, and for no good reason it just got worse. I wanted to be out of the house, but I was scared to be alone. No matter what I did, I couldn't concentrate except on questions such as "Am I going insane? What have I done to deserve this? What sort of punishment is this?"

You would think that if your circumstances were better, you would be too. But depression has a logic of its own. Once it settles in, it can't distinguish between a loving embrace, the death of a close friend, and the news that a neighbor's grass is growing.

Decisions? Impossible. The mind is locked. How can you choose? Nothing is working; the engine of your mind is barely turning over. And aren't most decisions emotional preferences? How can you decode when you *have* no emotional preferences?

Certainty? The only certainty is that misery will persist. If certainty of any good thing ever existed – and you can't remember when it did – it is replaced by constant doubt. You doubt that you are loved by anyone. You doubt your spouse's intentions. You doubt your spouse's fidelity. If you are a believer in Jesus Christ, you doubt the presence of Christ. You doubt the very foundation of your faith. "God have mercy on the man/Who doubts what he's sure of."[15]

The only thing you know is that you are guilty, shameful, and worthless. It is not that you have made mistakes in your life, or sinned, or reaped futility. It is that you *are* a mistake, you *are* sin, you *are* futility. "In this regard, depression can be a form of self-punishment, however subconsciously or involuntarily administered."[16] God has turned his back. Why bother going on in such a state? You might as well join God and turn your back on yourself too.

If forced to make distinctions, you might say that there are times that are worse than others, but who is able to measure different degrees of hell? Let's just say that there can be a rhythm to it. Asleep at 11:00 p.m., up at 2:00 a.m. Anguish, fears, and a torrent of pain lay hold of you while you try to live through the morning. It settles into the normal deep sadness and paralysis until mid-afternoon, and is followed by a steady drizzle of fear, pain, guilt, panic, deadness and fatigue until evening. Sometimes you might even reach the peaks of general malaise. It is true: the body can't take the pounding pain for too long. So you get some occasional breaks from the worst of it.

It can be quieter for some people. Instead of a bottomless abyss and howling in the brain, life is flat, gray, and cold.

---

[15] Bruce Springsteen, "Brilliant Disguise."

[16] W. Hulme and L. Hulme, *Wrestling with Depression: A Spiritual Guide to Reclaiming Life* (Minneapolis: Augsburg, 1995), p.22.

Nothing holds any interest. You are a barely walking zombie. Everything is drab, lifeless, and tired. Why work? Why get out of bed? Why do anything? Why commit suicide? Nothing seems to matter. You are afraid that if one of your children died, you *still* wouldn't feel anything.

Yet pain does break through in this more lifeless, numb state. It comes especially when you remember that you were once alive. Was it another person? Another lifetime? No, it must have been you. You remember that you actually wanted to have a sexual relationship with your spouse. A book on the shelf once kept you up all night; you couldn't put it down. That music would make you want to get up and dance. But you try to forget those times, because the contrast between then and now is almost unbearable. You prefer numbness.

It feels like you are always sick. In past generations or places less psychologically minded, they describe it solely in physical terms. For example, in China they call it *shenjing shuairo*, an alleged physical problem characterized by dizziness, fatigue, and headaches. Your body doesn't feel right. You are always tired. Doctors are consulted more than pastors or counselors.

In the early 1900s, a businessman reported these symptoms to his doctor.

> It's not just my body that's tired but my brain. I constantly feel as though an iron vise were tightening on my cranium. My head feels empty. My mind won't work. My ideas are confused and I can no longer concentrate. My memory is shot. When I read, I can't remember at the bottom of the page what I've read at the top. . . As for my will, my energy is gone. I no longer know what I want, what I'm supposed to do. I doubt, I hesitate, I don't dare make a decision.

25

Moreover, I've no appetite and I sleep badly. I have no sexual desire.[17]

How could this be all in my mind? he thinks.

You are waiting for a medical doctor to say that he made a mistake.

"The good news is that it's not all in your mind after all. I apologize for the misdiagnosis. The bad news is that the cancer will kill you in about a week and a half."

You are confident that everyone would be better off without you.

Is it any wonder that suicidal thoughts are always close?

Response

These descriptions might not sound hopeful, but they demonstrate that many others have gone through similar experiences. That in itself can be encouraging. You are not alone.

Also, many of these reflections were taken from people who were telling a larger story of hope and change. They are telling what *was* rather than what *is*. Most of them even had the mental energy and clarity to write moving and helpful literature.

What words would you choose? How would you describe the indescribable?

---

[17] Cited in Edward Shorter, *From the Mind to the Body: The Cultural Origins of Psychosomatic Symptoms* (New York: Free Press, 1994), p. 135.

CHAPTER 3

Definitions and Causes

While it is some encouragement to know that you are not alone and that others have experienced what you have, it is more helpful to know the cause and the cure. More than likely, you already have some suspicions about a cause for your depression.

Here is a suggestion: don't commit yourself too quickly to one explanation. Granted, it's something that begs for an answer, and there are more than enough interpretations from which to choose. But there are many causes of depression. Each individual depressive experience can have more than one cause. If you commit to one interpretation too soon, you can blind yourself to other important perspectives.

Types of Depression

Think of depression as a continuum of severity. On one end it is bothersome, at the other end debilitating. The less severe depression is technically called Dysthymic Disorder, the more severe, Major Depression. More popularly, the less severe is referred to as situational depression and the more severe as clinical depression (Figure 3.1).

27

▼LESS SEVERE

Situational Depression

Dysthymic Disorder

Discontent

▲MORE SEVERE

Clinical Depression

Major Depressive Disorder

Hopelessness

Figure 3.1. Levels of Depression.

The caretaker of the technical language for depression is the American Psychiatric Association (APA) and its diagnostic manual, the *Diagnostic and Statistical Manual of Mental Disorders*, now in its fourth edition (DSM-IV). It has proposed that the building block for "Depressive Disorder" or "Bipolar Disorder" is what the DSM-IV refers to as a "major depressive episode." It reads like this:

> Five (or more) of the following symptoms have been present during the same two-week period and represent a change from previous functioning; at least one of the symptoms is either (1) depressed mood or (2) loss of interest or pleasure.
> (1) depressed mood most of the day, nearly every day, as indicated by either subjective report (e.g., feels sad or empty) or observation made by others (e.g., appears tearful)
> (2) markedly diminished interest or pleasure in all, or almost all, activities most of the day, nearly every day
> (3) significant weight loss when not dieting or weight gain (e.g., a change of more than 5% of body

weight in a month), or decrease or increase in appetite nearly every day

(4) insomnia or hypersomnia nearly every day

(5) psychomotor agitation or retardation nearly every day (observable by others...)

(6) fatigue or loss of energy nearly every day

(7) feelings of worthlessness or excessive or inappropriate guilt... nearly every day...

(8) diminished ability to think or concentrate, or indecisiveness, nearly every day...

(9) recurrent thoughts of death..., recurrent suicidal ideation without a specific plan, or a suicide attempt or a specific plan for committing suicide... The symptoms are not due to the direct physiological effects of a substance (e.g., a drug of abuse, a medication) or a general medical condition (e.g., hypothyroidism).[1]

A Dysthymic Disorder is a variant of depression that lasts longer – at least two years – but is less intense. Instead of the longer symptom list of a Major Depressive Episode, the requirements for dysthymia omit some of the more severe criteria.

Presence, while depressed, of two (or more) of the following:

(1) poor appetite or overeating

(2) insomnia or hypersomnia

(3) low energy or fatigue

---

[1] American Psychiatric Association, *Diagnostic and Statistical Manual of Mental Disorders, Fourth Edition* (Washington, D.C.: American Psychiatric Association, 1994), p. 327.

(4) low self-esteem

(5) poor concentration or difficulty making decisions

(6) feelings of hopelessness[2]

Add to this list items such as feeling anxious, guilty, angry and unloved, and you can see how depression cuts such a broad swath that includes so many.

Over the last decade, an increasingly popular label for depression has been Bipolar Disorder. When those who are depressed are labeled Bipolar, it means that they probably experienced a period during which their mood was unusually elevated.

Types and Causes

Between the lines of these descriptions are all kinds of theories as to what causes them. As you move toward the less severe end of the continuum, many assume that the causes are relationship problems, difficult circumstances, or negative thinking. As you move toward the more severe end, the popular theory is that the cause is a chemical imbalance.

Don't buy into these generalizations just yet. Try instead to remain an agnostic for a little longer. At this point, it is too early to make those judgments. No one can confidently diagnose a chemical imbalance because there is no way to really know. Even if there were a test for it (which there isn't), the test couldn't tell you if the imbalance caused the depression or resulted from it.

The problem with immediately opting for a medical explanation is that, once the decision is made, every other perspective seems superficial or irrelevant. Why, for example,

---

[2] *Diagnostic and Statistical Manual of Mental Disorders, Fourth Edition*, p. 349.

would you bother considering issues raised by personal suffering when a pill might provide relief? If depressed persons assume that their problem is fundamentally medical, asking them to look at their relationships or their basic beliefs about God will seem as useful as prescribing physical exercise for baldness. Exercise is always helpful, but it won't grow hair.

One reason the previous chapter urges you to describe your feelings is that, as you do, you will begin to notice the fears, failures, losses, frustrations and broken relationships that might be attached to your feelings. When you see this patchwork of contributions, you can see that limiting yourself to a physical explanation might oversimplify your problem and cause you to miss road signs to other answers.

It is only fair to add that you should be an agnostic about spiritual causes too. You know that all types of hardships can challenge your faith. These hardships can strengthen your faith too, but you don't know much more than that. Some who are depressed strongly react against the suggestion of a possible spiritual cause. Others race toward the idea; they hope that once they discover the core sin, everything will change. They feel as if they must be spiritually deficient because they have no joy, no deep affection, no spiritual vitality. Maybe, they think, they are among the "lukewarm" of the book of Revelation (Rev. 3:16), a group they rightly would like to leave as soon as possible. But depression is a time to revisit both our own expectations and God's for our emotional life. Contrary to what we might think, God says that strong faith can coexist with emotional highs, lows, and everything in between. It is a myth that faith is always smiling. The truth is that faith often feels like the very ordinary process of dragging one foot in front of the other because we are conscious of God.

No sin is necessarily connected with sorrow of heart, for Jesus Christ our Lord once said, "My soul is exceedingly sorrowful, even to death." There was no sin in Him, and consequently none in His deep depression.[3]

At this point, here is what you know: Life is lifeless. Misery tinges everything. Your first reaction is, "How can I get rid of this as quickly as possible?" And there is merit to decreasing pain quickly, if it's possible. But depression should also be approached carefully. It might be pointing to important matters of the heart that are crying out for attention. Ignore them and they will just call back later. There are times when depression is saying something and we must listen.

Response

There will be some discussion about medication and other treatments in a later chapter. The concern at this point is not whether or not you are taking medication, but that medication does not become your only plan of attack. Even if medication relieves some of the burden of depression, it may be functioning like aspirin. That is, it takes away some of the symptoms but the root problems persist.

What else, other than chemical imbalances, might be contributing to your experience of depression?

---

[3] From C. H. Spurgeon, *Sword & Trowel*, 2000:1, p.11.

PART ONE   *Depression Is
Suffering*

CHAPTER 4

Suffering

With all the debate about the causes of depression, it is easy to miss the obvious: depression is painful. It is a form of suffering. At first, this statement seems to contribute nothing new. It is just restating what you already know. But if you are familiar with Scripture, you should sense a ray of light. Without Scripture's insights, suffering is random and senseless. When it comes, run fast! But Scripture is about suffering. It has given comfort to millions. It has spawned hundreds of wonderful books that highlight God's gentle care and Scripture's probing insights. The only problem we face is this: What words from God's rich communication to sufferers is most relevant?

If you search Scripture by looking up the word "depression" in a concordance, you would find only a short list of verses. (Depending on the translation, you might not find any list at all.) If you expand your investigation to include men and women whose struggles paralleled modern-day depression, you would find more material. Elijah, Saul, Jeremiah and Jonah are examples that immediately come to mind. But if your search includes the wider category of pain, suffering, hardship, trials, itions, despair, burdens, dread, hopelessness and a host of related words and themes, you will find that almost every page of Scripture offers some direction, insight, and encouragement.

For example, have you ever applied this teaching to depression?

> Consider it pure joy, my brothers, whenever you face trials of many kinds, because you know that the testing of your faith develops perseverance. Perseverance must finish its work so that you may be mature and complete, not lacking anything. (James 1:2-4)

These are not the easiest of God's words to hear, and it would take some explanation to link them to your situation. But the absence of the word "depression" shouldn't keep you from finding encouragement and purpose in this passage. James intentionally enlarges the scope of suffering – "trials of *many kinds*." By doing this, he invites those who experience depression to learn that, whatever the cause, depression will reveal our faith and serve as a catalyst for growth rather than a reason for despair.

This passage is just one randomly selected communication from God. Already you can see that there is purpose in suffering, and that, by itself, can have a profound impact on depression. "That is all I want in life: for this pain to seem purposeful."[1]

The Causes of Suffering

When depression is incorporated into the larger problem of

---

[1] Wurtzel, *Prozac Nation*, p. 50.

human suffering, you will find that you already know much more about depression than you realize. Scripture is like glasses for the color-blind and horribly near-sighted. With it, you will see details you didn't know existed and you will see them in Technicolor.

Turn Scripture's gaze, for example, to the question of what causes depression (suffering, trials). Its answers shun the simplistic and point to at least five possible causes.

Other people are one cause of hardship-depression. Look through the Psalms and you will find that about half of them are cries to the Lord because of oppression by others. People betray and abuse; they make commitments and break them; they wound, scatter, and destroy because they care about their own desires and not the interests of others. Beneath some depression you are likely to find a person who is reeling from the sins of other people.

We too are a cause of suffering. Our rage causes divorce and subsequent aloneness. Our stealing causes imprisonment. Don't be surprised if you find things within yourself – fears, anger and selfish desires – lurking behind some depression. Anger, especially, is a notorious cause.

Our bodies are another obvious cause of suffering. Since sin entered the world, our bodies gradually weaken and waste away. Diseases, deterioration from old age, post-partum struggles, and possible chemical imbalances are just a few of the physical causes relevant to depression.

This means that those we love will also suffer physical decline and death, which, of course, is another cause of personal pain and depression. The famous English preacher, Charles Spurgeon, struggled with depression throughout his life. What seems to have ignited it was a specific tragedy. He was preaching to a huge congregation – over twelve thousand crammed themselves into his church and over ten thousand waited outside. Soon after the meeting began, someone yelled, "Fire." In the chaos that ensued, the frantic crowd caused the death of seven people. Spurgeon was inconsolable.

These three causes – others, ourselves, and physical bodies that waste away and die – are obvious to the naked eye. But two other causes are harder to see without Scripture's lens and light.

Satan is a fourth cause of human suffering. The book of Job is one of the few places in Scripture where his work is obviously on display. Satan lies to us, he can afflict us physically, and he generally seeks to persuade us that allegiance to the true God is not in our best interests. Outside of religious circles, it isn't popular to talk about Satan, but that, in itself, is no reason to dismiss him. Satan doesn't seek name recognition; he prefers *not* to call attention to himself. Instead, he seeks to deflect attention away from God.

Finally, *God* himself is a cause of suffering. "God sometimes puts his children to bed in the dark," is the way an old preacher put it. We say that God "allows" suffering, and sometimes Scripture uses that language. But biblical authors were absolutely persuaded that God was the one, true, sovereign, Creator God. They could not imagine a world in which God was not enthroned. Nothing happened apart from his sovereign oversight, including our suffering.

> The LORD brings death and makes alive; he brings down to the grave and raises up. The LORD sends poverty and wealth; he humbles and he exalts. (1 Sam. 2:6-7)

> I [the LORD] form the light and create darkness, I bring prosperity and create disaster; I, the LORD, do all these things. (Isa. 45:7)

God is over all things, and nothing happens apart from his knowledge and will. By the time suffering or depression comes to our doorstep, God did it. To believe anything else is to opt for a universe that is random and out of control, without a guiding hand bringing all things to a purposeful and awe-inspiring conclusion.

This, of course, raises other questions about God's goodness, and those questions are on our agenda. For now, though, just orient yourself to seeing depression through the lens of suffering, and remember that suffering can come from a number of different causes. Don't jump to conclusions too quickly.

Multiple Causes

Having listed five possible causes for suffering, the next logical step is to discern the particular cause of a specific instance of suffering. But even that is not that simple. Although there are times when a particular cause is obvious, Scripture typically resists reducing hardships to a specific cause. Instead, for each struggle in our lives, it leads us to expect multiple causes.

A popular example is Joseph's hardship (Gen. 37-50). What began as sibling jealousy led to his abduction and sale as a slave by his own brothers. This was the first domino in a series of events that included betrayal by a lying woman and time in an Egyptian prison. When Joseph providentially encountered his brothers many years later, his explanation for his suffering was, "You [brothers] intended to harm me, but God intended it for good to accomplish what is now being done, the saving of many lives" (Gen. 50:20). In other words, Joseph identified two causes of his suffering: his brothers and God. In so doing, he opens a small window that provides glimpses of God's character. As Joseph understood it, God could be a cause of hardship, but in such a way that even the hardship evidenced his goodness. This, certainly, is a mystery, but Joseph is portrayed in Scripture as a wise person. He is a model whose perspective invites further reflection, which we will do in later chapters.

Another well known sufferer was the apostle Paul. His troubles were often caused by other people, but he too realized that God authored these sufferings to allow him to walk in the footsteps of Jesus and *his* sufferings. Among the more difficult trials was one he called his "thorn in the flesh" (2 Cor. 12:7). Although we never learn the precise nature of this malady, Paul identified at least three causes: his own pride, a messenger from Satan, and God – three causes for one hardship.

When applied to depression, this teaching suggests that our quest to find one specific cause could be too narrow. For example, depression might have a physical cause, but that doesn't exhaust the list of other possible contributions. It may simultaneously be a consequence of spiritual warfare, the sin of other people, and our own sin. And it is always under the oversight of the sovereign God.

Unknown Causes

Although Scripture reveals that there are multiple causes of suffering, and that multiple causes can be at work at any one time, it is less forthcoming about diagnosing the precise causes of particular hardships. Of course, there are times when the causes of our hardships are obvious. For example, if a friend suffers bankruptcy after years of accumulated gambling debts, he is the cause of his own suffering. If a woman leaves her spouse because she simply prefers her freedom, she is the cause of her suffering (and his). But even in these cases, we can't always discern the other factors that played a part, such as the person who introduced your friend to gambling, the bookie who kept extending credit, the co-worker who encouraged the wife to leave her husband, or the woman's mother, who casually divorced her husband and abandoned her family, thus modeling an option that the woman may have never considered otherwise.

The reason Scripture doesn't give clear guidelines for assigning responsibility is that it is not essential for us to know precise causes. Job, once again, is the model. Although we know that Satan caused Job's suffering, Job did not. Even after his fortunes were restored, he never knew why he suffered. Although he asked for an audience with God to plead his innocence, the only thing God revealed was that he is God and Job was not. Yet this more than satisfied all of Job's *why* questions.

Can you see a picture emerging? We might uncover some of the reasons for our suffering but we might never find them all. There is a mystery in suffering, just as there is ultimate mystery at the end of all human investigations.

Instead of teaching us how to identify the causes of suffering, Scripture directs us to the God who knows all things and is fully trustworthy. In other words, Scripture doesn't give us knowledge so that we will have intellectual mastery of certain events; it gives us knowledge so that we would know and trust God. "God, I don't know what you are doing, but you do, and that is enough." Somehow, turning to God and trusting him with the mysteries of suffering is the answer to the problem of suffering.

What does this have to do with depression? You might be able to discern some obvious causes of suffering, and knowing those causes might help alleviate the pain. But all suffering is intended to train us to fix our eyes on the true God. Therefore, depression, regardless of the causes, is a time to answer the deepest and most important of all questions: Whom will I trust? Whom will I worship?

Response

This is a lot to take in at one time. You are seeing how a simple inclusion of depression into the larger category of suffering has immense implications. Your response, however, might be less than enthusiastic. On the one hand, you know that there is hope for sufferers. Tens of thousands have grown through their hardships and bear testimony that God is faithful. But this still raises the age-old questions: How could God allow such a painful, life-draining event in your life? How could such a God care? How could he be good?

There are two ways to ask these questions. One is with a clenched fist; the other is with an open heart. The first person doesn't want to hear any answers, the other is listening. If you are listening, these are good questions to ask because there are answers.

What difference does it make when you see your own struggle with depression as a form of suffering?

CHAPTER 5

God

There are paradoxes in most depression.

You loathe the isolation of depression, but you avoid other people.

You want help, but you don't always listen.

You believe there is a God, but you feel like an atheist.

Since the paradox regarding God is arguably the most important, let's look at this one first. You will find it in all kinds of suffering.

You have heard it said that there are no atheists in foxholes. During times of intense crisis, many people who have never had a religious thought are suddenly, with all humility, praying, reciting the Lord's prayer, and remembering, "The Lord is my shepherd..." as if these things were encoded in all human DNA.

But if the problems soon disappear, so do thoughts about God. The warrior goes on his or her way without a word of thanks, let alone long-term faithfulness. But what if the battle continues and circumstances don't change? The humble pleas become questions that might not be angry but at least are bold. "Why, God, are you doing this to me?" "What have I ever done to you?" Suffering nags us with questions about God in a way that comfort never could.

When dire circumstances continue their assault, you might notice the paradox of being an "atheistic believer." If you were pushed to decide, you would say that God exists, yet you feel increasingly isolated and alone. The more extreme the suffering, the more intense is the sense of aloneness. *If God exists*, you think, *it certainly doesn't feel like he does.* "During my deepest depression I had no faith,"[1] is the refrain, even among those who have had obvious faith. A French psychiatrist, after years of seeing depressed patients, observed, "All depressed people are sullen, radical atheists." Whatever side of the paradox is emphasized in your own life – believer or unbeliever – depression raises questions about God. They are unavoidable during any kind of prolonged suffering.

There is much discussion about the ways in which depressed people have distorted and inaccurate thinking, but here – in their spiritual wrestlings, questions, and practical atheism – they are onto something. At its very roots, life is about God. Whether you shake your fist at him, consider him so distant that his existence is irrelevant, or tremble before him because you feel that you are under his judgment, the reality is this: the basic questions of life and the fundamental issues of the human heart are about God. Life is about knowing him or avoiding him. It is about spiritual allegiances. Whom will you trust in the midst of pain? Whom will you worship?

Consider Job again. The intense suffering and great loss in his life drove him immediately to a basic spiritual question. Now that suffering was a resident in his home, would he still trust and worship God?

---

[1] W. Hulme and L. Hulme, *Wrestling with Depression: A Spiritual Guide to Reclaiming Life* (Minneapolis: Augsburg, 1995), p.45.

His answer was unambiguous. When he lost all his children, "he fell to the ground in worship," and made a shocking declaration. "The Lᴏʀᴅ gave and the Lᴏʀᴅ has taken away; may the name of the Lᴏʀᴅ be praised" (Job 1:21).

At this moment you may not feel like falling to the ground in worship. Numbness, pain, and worship don't seem to go together. But at least consider who God is. Depression both requires this and avoids it. It requires it because all suffering leads to questions about the character of God, but it avoids it because no one naturally pursues God. Suffering makes him seem all the more distant and disinterested.

As you consider God, expect to find fallacies in your thinking about yourself and God. In other words, although you may think that you know all you need to know about God – or all you want to know – you don't. If you resist such an offer, you are probably angry with God, in which case it is all the *more* reason to consider who he is. He invites angry people to come and be surprised.

Surprise #1: Jesus shared in our sufferings

There is a strange split we sometimes make between Jesus and God the Father. The Father is always a little testy and picky with our faults; Jesus is always kind and forgiving. The triune God, however, is one God, and he has chosen to most fully reveal himself in Jesus. Jesus is God's summary of himself. "The Son is the radiance of God's glory and the exact representation of his being" (Heb. 1:3).

Jesus is the most sophisticated expression of God's person to us. In him you can take your pick of what is surprising. Here is one: Jesus shared in our sufferings.

If you invented a religious system, it's unlikely that you would imagine a god who became like the people he created. But God did even more. He became like his creatures *and* willingly suffered a horrifying death so that they could be spared. Even the men and women who studied Scripture didn't anticipate that God would come this close. They never guessed that the Messiah, God himself, would suffer in the way he did.

If you think God is far away and indifferent, here is the surprising revelation. From the foundation of the world, God knew your sufferings and declared that he himself would take human form and participate in them (which means that we too could share in his). This is not a distant, indifferent God.

In an African hospital, a pastor who had just witnessed another death was approached by a poor, elderly woman.

> "You know," she said, taking my [the pastor's] arm, "through many losses of family and friends and through much sorrow, the Lord has taught me one thing. Jesus Christ did not come to take away our pain and suffering, but to share in it."[2]

Just one chapter of Scripture (Mark 14), chronicling only one day, reveals the extent to which Jesus shared our sufferings.

> The chief priests and teachers of the law were looking for a sly way to arrest Jesus and kill him. (v. 1)
> Judas agreed to betray Jesus for a fee.
> Jesus predicted that one of his followers would deny any knowledge of him.
> Jesus predicted that his other followers would abandon him.
> The leaders arrested him.

[2] K. Sempangi, *A Distant Grief* (Ventura, Cal.: Regal, 1979), p. 179.

He was spit on.

He was struck with fists and beaten to the point where he could have died from the lashings alone.

And this was *before* he was shamed and crucified.

Yet it was the LORD's will to crush him [Jesus] and cause him to suffer. (Isa. 53:10)

He then began to teach them that the Son of Man must suffer many things and be rejected by the elders, chief priests and teachers of the law, and that he must be killed and after three days rise again. (Mark 8:31)

In bringing many sons to glory, it was fitting that God, for whom and through whom everything exists, should make the author of their salvation perfect through suffering. (Heb 2:10)

He was called "man of sorrows" (Isa. 53:3). He was oppressed, afflicted, despised and rejected, to the point where people would turn away to avoid seeing his face. You know these things about Jesus, but now that you, too, are familiar with suffering, it should shock you that anyone would voluntarily take such suffering on himself.

Sufferers should be able to recognize other sufferers. As a sufferer, you should recognize Jesus' sufferings; he certainly recognizes yours. A deep sigh gives it away. When Jesus healed a deaf man, he let out a deep sigh as he looked up to heaven (Mark 7:34). He was moved by the suffering he saw around him, and as the risen Lord he continues to be moved by ours today.

Martin Luther said that the cross alone is our theology. At the cross we see that God took the suffering and judgment on himself. Look closely and you will see an innocent lamb slaughtered. As a result, theologians have been quick to note that what happens to the sinful creatures of God, however tragic, is less monstrous and criminal than what happened to the Son of God.[3]

How can you respond?

• Have you noticed that sometimes, in the presence of someone whose suffering seems greater than our own, our suffering seems lighter, less intense? It is as if the suffering of another can temporarily take us out of ourselves. The sufferings of Jesus can, indeed, elevate us and take us out of ourselves.

• The cross says that life will not be easy. If Jesus serves, we will serve. If Jesus suffers, we too will experience hardships. No servant is greater than the master. Yet things are not always the way they appear. Suffering is part of the path that leads to glory and beauty. "He who goes out weeping, carrying seed to sow, will return with songs of joy, carrying sheaves with him" (Ps. 126:6). Suffering has a purpose. It is changing us so that we look more and more like Jesus himself. "When Christ calls a man, he bids him come and die."[4] But that death is not the end of the story.

• When someone has suffered like you, they understand you before you speak. They can even supply words that describe your suffering. Jesus suffered; therefore, he knows our suffering.

[3] P. T. Forsyth, *The Justification of God* (London: Independent Press, 1917), p. 149.

[4] D. Bonhoeffer, *The Cost of Discipleship* (New York: Macmillan, 1967), p. 99.

Surprise #2: God is good and generous

It is hard to argue when we are reminded that Jesus shared in our sufferings and has compassion for those who suffer. It is easier to protest, however, when we hear the proposition that God is both good and generous. At this moment in your life, it would seem that goodness and generosity, especially from the all-powerful God, could only be demonstrated by a removal of the depression. If he takes it away, you are persuaded. If not, you remain a doubter.

But remember what you already know. First, Jesus suffered, and Jesus was dearly loved as the only Son of the Father. When we suffer what seems like endless pain, it is hard to believe that God loves us, but Jesus' suffering proves that it can be true. That doesn't mean that we always understand what is going on behind the scenes, but it is true nonetheless. Somehow, temporary suffering and love can go together.

Second, "he who did not spare his own Son, but gave him up for us all – how will he not also, along with him, graciously give us all things?" (Rom. 8:32). The cross is the only evidence that can fully persuade you that God is, at all times, good and generous. There is no arguing with someone who is willing to make this ultimate sacrifice. If someone gives his only child for you, you can't doubt that person's love. When the memory of such a costly sacrifice becomes distant, and life's frustrations tempt us to doubt, all we need is a quick reminder. Our God says, "If I have sacrificed my Son for you, do you really think I am going to be stingy and withhold my love now?"

When children don't get what they want when they want it, they have a hard time believing that their parents truly love them. After all, what could be better than satisfying all their wants? But parents know about a more sophisticated love.

They know that catering to their children's wishes is not always in their children's best interests. Sometimes they should eat broccoli. Sometimes it is best for them to go to bed, even though their friends are still outside playing. But just try to persuade children of your love at those times! All you can do is remind them that you love them. "My child, you know that I love you and want only the best for you. I know that what I am doing now could seem mean, but think about it. You know that I never want to be cruel to you. I love you. You will have to trust that I love you this time, because I know it doesn't feel that way."

God is good and he is generous. He is not stingy. He commands his people not to covet because it is a form of denying his generosity. He is not trying to hold out on you until you are whipped into shape. Demons would have you believe such things. Instead, he says, "Open wide your mouth and I will fill it" (Ps. 81:10). He invites us to the most lavish of banquets, and all he requires is that we are hungry and bring nothing (Isa. 55:1-3).

This is not a religious attempt to drum up some good feelings. It *is* harder to be surprised by the goodness and generosity of God when you feel so miserable. Of the Puritan William Cowper it was said, "It is possible to be a child of God, without consciousness of the blessing, and to have title to a crown, and yet feel to be immured in the depths of a dungeon."[5] The goal is simply to remind you of the truth. Your job is simply to believe (John 6:29).

Response
What have been your responses to these ideas? Pay attention

---

[5] "William Cowper and His Affliction," *The Banner of Truth*, Issue 96, Sept. 1971, p. 28.

to them. Indifference? Ambivalence? A glimmer of hope? Hostility? Does it seem like talk about stars and galaxies when all you want is to get your car fixed?

What is your response saying? What is it revealing about you?

Are you a fair weather friend who trusts God during the good times but becomes more suspicious in the hard times? If so, welcome to the human race. Set your sights on someone like St. Basil. Gregory of Nyssa remarked that his faith was "ambidextrous" – he welcomed pleasure on one hand and affliction on the other.

You must do battle at this point with depression's tendencies toward passivity. Don't wait to have faith inserted into your heart. Seek the Lord. If there is any guarantee in Scripture, it is that he will reveal more and more of himself to those who seek him. Read the great prayers of Scripture (Eph. 1:17-23; 3:14-19) and make them your own.

CHAPTER 6

Cry Out to the Lord

Have you ever been to a church service in which the order and content of the service were prescribed from start to finish? These are called liturgical services. They consist of prayers and readings that have been prepared in advance.

If you are depressed, you are going to have to learn to be a liturgical worshiper.

If you wait until you feel motivated to worship, you might be waiting a long time. If you are remotely inclined to communicate with God, you might find that words fail and you have nothing to say. When you drag yourself to worship, the service had better be mapped out ahead of time.

Depression Bends Inward

Everything turns inward in depression. A beautiful flower momentarily catches your attention, but within seconds the focus bends back into your own misery. You see loved ones who are celebrating a recent blessing, but before you can synchronize your feelings with theirs, you have doubled back to your own personal emptiness. Like a boomerang that always returns, no matter how hard you try, you can't get away from yourself.

Pain is like that. If any part of your body is injured, you can't get away from the pain. You may have brief distractions, but then the throbbing breaks through your consciousness and dominates again. At its peak, there seems to be no way out. You feel trapped by it.

Alternatives are few. You could try fighting, but that just earns you a few more seconds of distraction. So you just try to survive the day.

Two Choices

But there are other alternatives. More accurately, there are choices. You are standing at a crossroads and you will take one path or another. There is no such thing as not choosing, because "not choosing" is one of the paths. It too is a choice.

Your decision is between calling out to the Lord or not. This is the choice that has confronted those in misery throughout history. Listen to the prophet Hosea, who wrote these words on behalf of the Lord: "They do not cry out to me from their hearts but wail upon their beds" (Hos. 7:14).[1] You can sit in silence or cry to the Lord. You can cry on your bed or cry to the Lord. These are the two choices.

Now you can see why liturgical prayers might be very useful. When you try to call out to the Lord, you have no words. You don't have words to describe your experience; you don't have words to bless God; and you don't even know what to request. This would seem to doom you to silence if it weren't for the fact that God is pleased to communicate with his people. He delights in teaching us how to call out to him.

---

[1] Thanks to Andree Seu, who pointed out this passage to me.

God Names the Silences

God might feel far away, but our feelings mislead us on this one. Scripture is filled with promises of God's presence with his people. Do you want evidence? God speaks to us, and desires to be spoken to. Only someone close can do such things. He speaks to us, especially through Scripture, and he calls us to speak with him. When we are tongue-tied, he actually gives us words to say.

Yet it is not a script that he gives us. When we speak from a script, we are pretending. We wear the mask of another. We become actors. Instead, God gives us poetry that, somehow, gives voice to the silences in our hearts. If we had the skill and the words, we would write many of those same words.

The Psalms are where you find many of these poems. They are God's liturgy, prepared for you in advance.

> How long, O LORD? Will you forget me forever?
> How long will you hide your face from me? (Ps. 13:1)

> I am a worm and not a man. (Ps. 22:6)

> My heart is in anguish within me; the terrors of death assail me. Fear and trembling have beset me; horror has overwhelmed me. I said, "Oh, that I had the wings of a dove! I would fly far away and be at rest – I would flee far away and stay in the desert." (Ps. 55:4-7)

> I sink in the miry depths, where there is no foothold. I have come into the deep waters; the floods engulf me. I am worn out calling for help; my throat is parched. My eyes fail, looking for my God. (Ps. 69:2-3)

My soul is full of trouble and my life draws near the grave.... You have put me in the lowest pit, in the darkest depths.... But I cry to you for help, O LORD; in the morning my prayer comes before you. Why, O LORD, do you reject me and hide your face from me? (Ps. 88:3, 6, 13-14)

Begin a search. Start with words and phrases that reflect your experience. If that seems too much, ask someone to read selected psalms to you.

Don't forget that, although these psalms are expressing very raw emotions, they are words that God himself is giving you. He is the minister who has arranged the order of service. He is the father who is teaching you how to speak.

The Psalms of Jesus

When you hear the words of Psalm 22, "My God, why have you forsaken me?," you might think about your own experience. Depression feels like being forsaken. But you also remember that these were Jesus' words on the cross. They point to the fact that when you read these liturgical prayers, you are not alone. David composed many of them, the Israelites sang them, the church has recited them, and they all point to Jesus. Ultimately, they are all his songs and you are being taught to sing with him. Jesus is the Divine Singer, and now the songs of the Son of God have been given as gifts to the children of God.

What these psalms do is straighten the trajectory of our lives. Using the words he gives us, God gently turns our hearts toward him. Instead of everything bending back into ourselves, we are able to look straight, outside of ourselves, and fix our eyes on Jesus (Heb. 12:2).

Keep this pattern in mind. It is the path of hope. The fact

that all your thoughts turn back on yourself is oppressive. The self cannot carry the load. The way we were intended to function was to be able to look outward, toward God and other people. As you say the Psalms and remember that Jesus said them first, you will gradually find your focus changing. Perhaps you will notice it in the way you greet someone before she greets you; perhaps you will start writing some of your own prayers. Step by step you will emerge from your isolated darkness.

Try Entire Psalms

As you make the words of Jesus your own, try working with larger portions of individual psalms. This will allow you to recite words about your own experience and about God. For example, Psalm 22 begins with an honest expression of the heart: "Why have you forsaken me?" This is a statement of faith because you are saying it to God. You know enough about his character that it makes no sense to you to feel so forsaken. But when you sing the larger psalm, it will guide you to a new place.

> He has not despised or disdained the suffering of the afflicted one; he has not hidden his face from him but has listened to his cry for help. (v. 24)

> The poor will eat and be satisfied; they who seek the LORD will praise him…. All the ends of the earth will remember and turn to the LORD, and all the families of the nations will bow down before him, for dominion belongs to the LORD and he rules over the nations. (vv. 26-28)

Hope, as you will find, is a skill that takes practice. There is no verse, pill, or possession that will make it magically appear.

Reciting psalms that you have claimed as your own is part of that practice.

Call Out Often

When you go to a liturgical service, there are times when your heart feels revived and full of life. You recite the Scripture and prayers with great passion. At other times you might feel as if you are going through the motions, but you say the prayers and read the Scripture because the words are true. God hears them, and he is pleased that you are crying out to him, however feebly it may seem, rather than wailing on your bed. "The prayers offered in the state of dryness are those which please him best."[2]

Faith feels many different ways. It can be buoyant; it can be depressed and lifeless. Feelings don't define faith. Instead, faith is simply turning to the Lord. When you speak the psalms, you are "doing" faith. And remember that faith is the work of the Spirit of God in our hearts. As such, if you can speak psalms, God is near.

With this in mind, persevere. Don't just speak the prayers so that your depression can lift. Speak them because they are true and because they are evidence of Christ at work in you. Speak them often.

> I have posted watchmen on your wall, O Jerusalem; they will never be silent day or night. You who call on the LORD, give yourselves no rest, and give him no rest till he establishes Jerusalem and makes her the praise of the earth. (Isa. 62:6-7)

---

[2] C. S. Lewis, The *Screwtape Letters* (New York, Macmillan, 1977), p. 39.

Say your liturgy at set times during the day. Get others to pray with you and for you.

Response

Maybe you feel like a spiritual misfit because you can't own an entire psalm. As soon as you are connected to it, it moves off into spiritual heights and leaves you behind. If you can stay with parts of it, that is more than enough for now. Faith is not the presence of warm religious feeling. It's the knowledge that you walk before the God who hears. Read Psalm 88. Notice how it ends with "darkness is my closest friend." We don't think of this as an expression of faith, but, when you say it to the God who hears it, it is heroic faith.

Let me remind you where we are. We have not yet delved into the specifics of your depression. Instead, we are just touching on some of God's communication to you. Please don't think that we are going to exhaust Scripture's depths. Instead, be encouraged that God's words of comfort and direction are nearly limitless. Scores of wonderful books only begin to unwrap Scripture's surprises.

If nothing resonates with you, then consider why. Sometimes we want God to be distant. Although your indifference could come from other places, isn't it true that we are indifferent when we no longer want to bother with someone? Perhaps you have unvoiced frustrations in your relationship with God. What might they be? Speak them to him.

> Trust in him at all times, O people:
>> pour out your heart to him,
>> for God is our refuge. (Ps. 62:8)

CHAPTER 7

Warfare

If you knew an enemy was in hot pursuit, you would be on guard, especially if that enemy specialized in guerrilla tactics. Even when depressed, a threat on our lives is enough to ensure a surge of energy, unless, of course, we didn't know an enemy was after us.

During times of suffering and difficulty, spiritual warfare is virtually guaranteed. We watch Satan seize what he thought was his golden opportunity when Jesus was led into the desert to endure physical suffering and spiritual isolation (Matt. 4). How much more will Satan pursue mere mortals when they go through the emotionally arid experience of depression? The Bible depicts him as a lion, lurking in the tall grass, patiently waiting to devour those who are susceptible (1 Peter 5:8).

Think about the nature of depression. Life is turned inward. You already have a sense that, for all practical purposes, God is not present. Add to that your relentless condemnation and pervasive self-criticism, which have persuaded you that God doesn't love you. You couldn't be a more obvious spiritual target if you painted a bull's-eye on your chest.

Satan's Strategies

Satan masquerades as an angel of light (2 Cor. 11:14), which means that he is not easily noticed. But the apostle Paul assures us that God has revealed enough to make us aware of his schemes and tactics (2 Cor. 2:11). To identify them, we should be thinking about the common and ordinary more than the bizarre. Overt demon possession, with its frightening manifestations, is one of Satan's tactics, but it also doubles as a ploy to have us think that his strategies are *always* accompanied by signs that draw attention to him. The truth is that, for his day-to-day business, he prefers not to alarm. He works more subtly in the following ways.

Lies. Is there anything more common and ordinary than lies? They certainly don't capture our attention any more, because they come so naturally to us. Young children lie without being taught. Politicians lie and we expect it. The variations are endless: white lies, whoppers, self-justifications, exaggerations, minimizing, changing the subject.

Behind these deceptions is something more than an attempt to duck personal responsibility for wrongdoing. Behind them is the father of lies, Satan himself. "When he lies, he speaks his native language, for he is a liar and the father of lies" (John 8:44).

You too are vulnerable. You might be loyal to beliefs that are wrong but highly resistant to change. For example, since you *feel* like you are a burden to your family and you *feel* like they would be better off without you, you *believe* that is the truth. All their protests and expressions of love will not persuade you to change your mind. If you *feel* that God has abandoned you, then you believe that he actually has. Nothing will persuade you otherwise. In other words, feelings can lie.

Do you see the progression?

You are spiritually vulnerable ⟶ your emotions are so powerful that they skew your interpretations ⟶ Satan attacks ⟶ you swear allegiance to your most pessimistic interpretation no matter what others say.

There are no incantations, spinning heads, strange voices, or obvious satanic rituals involved here. It all seems very natural. But this is knock-down, drag-out spiritual warfare.

Lies About Us. Satan's lies are calculated and strategic. They are directed at the spiritual jugular – the most important issues of life.

Do you believe that some things you have done are too bad to be forgiven? If so, you are believing Satan's lie that the blood of Jesus can only handle little or unintentional sins. The truth is that, through the cross, the judgment for sin has been taken by Christ for those who believe, including yourself if you have claimed faith in Jesus.

Do you believe that it is impossible for the Holy God to love you and even delight in you? If so, you are believing Satan's lie that God loves you because of what you do. The truth is that he loves you because he is the God who loves, and the sacrifice of Jesus proves it. The cross of Christ expresses God's delight in all who believe, and if you believe that Jesus is the risen Lord, he delights in and loves you.

Do you believe that you have no reason to live? If so, you are believing Satan's lie that you belong only to yourself. The truth is that you belong to God and you have a God-given purpose. Furthermore, the cross of Christ reveals that God's purposes for your life are *good.*

Do you believe that these questions are unimportant? If so, you are believing Satan's lie that our relationship with God is unrelated to our struggle with depression. The truth is that your relationship with God is absolutely necessary, especially now.

Your life depends on it.

Waver on these questions and you will be experiencing the battle.

Don't think that these lies are automatically downloaded into our minds where we robotically replay them. Lies don't just impose themselves on our hearts. Instead, Satan's lies come to us after the seeds already exist. He is the counselor who endorses the lies we already suspect are true. He is the false witness who is quick to confirm our false interpretation. This is why spiritual warfare seems so natural. We are not being taken against our wills. Rather than fight us where we have strong faith and certainty and lies will seem silly and obvious, Satan looks for faith that is weak in the hopes that we will meekly surrender. It begins when we harbor doubts. Satan, ever the opportunist, sees vulnerability and simply says, "Yes, what you believe is true."

Lies About God. If you look carefully at the lies you believe, you will notice that you are caught in a cross-fire. Yes, you are an intended casualty and the lies are self-condemning, but you are not the primary target of those lies. Instead, the volleys are aimed especially at the character of God. Their goal is to raise questions about God. Specifically, they question God's love and power.

Notice, for example, Satan's initial lies: "Did God really say, 'You must not eat from any tree in the garden? '" (Gen. 3:1). "'You will not surely die'" (3:4).

These words directly attack the goodness and truthfulness of God, which are both expressions of love. Satan is saying, "Can God's words really be trusted?" "Is God really good?" "Perhaps he is just holding out on you." "Perhaps he is stingy." With these questions and accusations, he has all the firepower he needs. Most spiritual warfare consists of minor variations on these age-old assaults.

So if you suspect that you are vulnerable to Satan's lies – and, if you are depressed, just assume you are – rephrase those lies and see that they are more about God than they are about you.

For example, "I am worthless" could be reinterpreted as, "God has not given me the success I desired; therefore, I don't believe that he is good."

"I have lost the most important thing in life" could be reinterpreted as "God is not enough."

"I can't go on" becomes "I don't believe that God hears or is powerful enough to work through human weakness."

Can you see it? Our suffering may come from many different places, but, regardless of its origin, Satan ultimately is a player. Suffering is the ideal time for him to raise questions about God, because we ourselves are already asking them. Suffering raises spiritual questions that cannot be ignored. The apostle Paul underscores this when he reminds us that, during suffering, demonic warfare "sets itself up against the knowledge of God" (2 Cor. 10:5).

Lies that focus on temporal, not spiritual realities. This popular deception is underway even before suffering begins. During the better times, Satan happily encourages us to see the goodness of God all around us.

"You have a strong marriage? Isn't God good!"

"Your health is fine? Isn't God good!"

"Your bills are paid and there is some money in the bank? Isn't God good!"

"Train your eye on these earthly blessings, and gauge God's goodness by what you see, because life will not always be an accumulation of good things. Then, when the hardships come, you will look out and have no evidence of God's goodness."

This is what Satan tried, albeit unsuccessfully, with Job. Job had all the best things in life, and Satan assumed that once they were gone, Job would turn his back on God. But Job trusted in God throughout, causing Satan to flee.

Our Counterattack

If you want to follow in Job's footsteps, you have the spiritual advantage over Satan. In fact, you have more of an advantage than Job did. Job didn't know what we know about Satan. Job wasn't preceded by Jesus, who stood firm against Satan in the wilderness. What happens in our lives when we simply say to Jesus, "Yes, I trust you," is that we also trust in his power to stand firm against Satan's attacks.

The details of how faith works in spiritual warfare are well known but easily forgotten.

Remember that you have an enemy. Follow the lead of wise people who begin each day by actually saying, "Today, I must be alert that I have an enemy." Ask others to remind you, and be quick to remind others. Realize that you are walking where rebels are known to be in the area. Their lives are devoted to your destruction.

Assume that warfare rages. Don't even bother looking for signs of warfare. Just assume that you are in the thick of it. If you want evidence, don't look for it in the intensity of your depression. We don't know if Satan has a hand in your depression itself, but we do know that he will use the chronic nature of your pain as a venue to employ well-worn strategies like these:

Are you hopeless? Do you believe God is aloof and distant?
Do you question God's love?
Do you question God's forgiveness?
Do you see no point in knowing Christ better? Remember

that Satan will always attack the character of God.

Are you listening to wise counsel and Scripture? If not, it is a sure sign that you are losing some spiritual skirmishes. Listening is a mark of humility, and Satan can't successfully fight against it.

Don't think that your case is unique. This popular lie questions God's care: all sufferers are tempted to believe that their suffering is unique. This lie immediately renders all counsel irrelevant because no one understands and no advice applies. The result is that the aloneness you already experience is now an established fact, and you are given ever more permission to despair.

No one is immune from this lie, and everyone can give personal examples of its attraction. For example, William Cowper was a popular eighteenth century hymn writer who wrote lyrics such as "There is a fountain filled with blood." Although he was immersed in Scripture, he reported of his depression, "There is no encouragement in the Scripture so comprehensive as to include my case, nor any consolation so effectual as to reach it."[1]

With depression, assume the lie is present. Consider it a permanent attachment. As long as you struggle with depression, you will have to be particularly alert to it. Your goal isn't to overcome it; your goal is to engage it with a growing knowledge of Jesus Christ.

Know Christ. Satan's energies zero in on one point: the truth about Jesus. If you are growing in an accurate knowledge of Jesus Christ, you are winning the battle. If you are not, you are losing ground daily.

The knowledge of Christ is revealed most fully at the cross —

---

[1] "William Cowper and His Affliction," *The Banner of Truth*, Issue 96, Sept. 1971, p.28.

the death and resurrection of Jesus, the thing of first importance (1 Cor. 15:3-5). The cross is the evidence that Christ's love is much more than good intentions or compassion without action. It shows us that Christ's love was a holy love that surpasses our understanding. If we are angry that God allows depression in our lives, we should be reminded that his love is much more sophisticated than we know. Our anger shows that we are small children who think we know what is best.

It is no surprise that the knowledge of Christ is central to God's plan for everything, not just spiritual warfare. God has exalted Christ over all things. When we know and honor Jesus, God is pleased to bless us with more: more knowledge, more faith, more love, more hope. We are thus better equipped to fight.

Another reason it is so important to know Jesus is that one of the grand purposes of human existence is to look more and more like him. This is God's plan for us. It is one of the greatest gifts he could give. It is evidence that he has brought us into his family. If Jesus learned obedience through suffering, we will too. A path *without* hardships should cause us to wonder if we really belong to God.

The challenge for us is to think as God thinks. In other words, our present thinking must be turned upside-down. We once thought that suffering was to be avoided at all costs; now we must understand that the path to becoming more like Jesus goes through hardship, and it is much better than the path of brief and superficial comfort without Jesus. When we understand this grand purpose, we discover that suffering does not oppose love; it is a result of it (Heb. 12:8). We are under the mistaken impression that divine love cannot coexist with human pain. Such thinking is one of Satan's most effective strategies.

It must be attacked with the gospel of grace.

Humble yourself before the Lord. When you are depressed, you feel like you can't be any lower. But an appropriate and strengthening response to the love of Christ is humility. Humility is different from feeling low. It is lowering ourselves *before* God, and accepting his sovereign will.

Humility says, "God owes me nothing." "He is not my servant; I am his." "God is God, and he has the right to do anything he wants."

This is the gift God gave Job in Job's spiritual battle. Whereas Job wanted to question God, he was instead questioned *by* God, and after hearing God's fatherly questions, Job was humbled before him. "'I am unworthy – how can I reply to you? I put my hand over my mouth'" (Job 40:4). When you have a growing knowledge of God, your natural response is humility. In the face of such a powerful spiritual response to the knowledge of Christ, Satan is powerless.

Response

Consider your response to spiritual warfare. Do you know that it rages even though you are not emotionally moved by that knowledge? Then you are on the path. The Spirit is at work in your life.

Now take some small steps to engage in the struggle. Consider reading Job 38-42. The questions might seem harsh, but realize that this is the way Hebrew fathers taught their children. The context is love.

Does this discussion seem irrelevant? If so, you will want to consider two questions. First, *is your allegiance to Jesus Christ?* If it isn't, be open to knowing Jesus. How could you refuse an opportunity to consider a person who promises life and hope? If you are not sure of your allegiances, do the same thing. Be

71

open to knowing him better. There are ways that you will know Jesus in your suffering that are unique and profound.

If you have publicly voiced your faith in Jesus but now are filled with doubts, can you distinguish between depression and faith? Don't forget that depression casts its shadow on everything, even faith. As a result, faith won't feel jubilant. But that doesn't mean you don't or can't believe. That is your job. Jesus said, "The work of God is this: to believe in the one he has sent" (John 6:29). Say, "Amen" when someone speaks the truth to you. Begin your day with "Yes, Lord, I believe," however weak your faith may be.

The other question to consider is this: *Do you want to change?* As bizarre as it might seem, depression can come to feel like a friend. You wouldn't choose this friend if you had a choice, but now that you have him, he is comfortable and predictable. You can even derive personal identity from him, which is especially tempting when you feel like you have no identity without him. If you are not engaging in the spiritual battle we have discussed so far, it is possible that you are deceiving yourself. Perhaps you are merely going through the motions. Then you can say that you have tried when you haven't, and you can have a clear conscience when you remain entrenched in your hopelessness.

This is a battle. If you want change, you must be willing to take yourself to task.

CHAPTER 8

Remember

Show a favorite toy to a very young child, then quickly put it behind your back. It demonstrates that you possess magical powers, at least from the child's perspective. You have just made a solid object vanish!

Now put the toy in front of the child again. Abracadabra, poof, magic! It reappeared out of nowhere.

Of course, you can't take any credit for this sleight of hand. You are simply taking advantage of a brain that is still maturing. Very young children think the object has disappeared; older children will look behind your back for the hidden toy. For them, it may still be a game, but it is no longer magic. It's a phenomenon called object permanence – the ability to know that a hidden object still exists although we can't see it. It is an ability we grow into.

Spiritual reality is like that. You hear a great illustration, you participate in a Christ-centered worship service, and your heart is moved. But within minutes, it is as if you never heard a word and never participated. You leave the same way you entered – a case of spiritual Alzheimer's. You don't even hear an echo. It is as though we have not yet reached the stage of object permanence, at least when it comes to the knowledge of God.

With this in mind, Scripture beseeches us to remember. Before Jesus came, Scripture offered many mnemonic devices, such as yearly feasts that celebrated God's deliverance and Scripture that could be read daily. Since Jesus' death and resurrection, God is willing to jog your memory day after day. Scripture is more accessible, we celebrate the Lord's Supper, and we are given the Holy Spirit, who testifies as an eyewitness and continually points us to Christ. God, apparently, is happy to repeat himself.

For some people, repetition becomes a been-there-done-that and they check out until there is something new. For the wise, however, remembering is essential to the human soul. It is part of that forsaken art of meditating. It is critical to the process of change, and a prominent means of doing spiritual battle.

Here is a psalm that can guide your remembering.

> Out of the depths I cry to you, O LORD;
>> O Lord, hear my voice.
>> Let your ears be attentive to my cry for mercy.
> If you, O LORD, kept a record of sins,
>> O Lord, who could stand?
> But with you there is forgiveness;
>> therefore you are feared.
> I wait for the LORD, my soul waits,
>> and in his word I put my hope.
> My soul waits for the Lord
>> more than watchmen wait for the morning,
>> more than watchmen wait for the morning.
> O Israel, put your hope in the LORD,
>> for with the LORD is unfailing love

and with him is full redemption.
He himself will redeem Israel from all their sins.
(Ps. 130)

Out of the Depths

Psalm 130 begins with sufferings that have pulled the psalmist into the vortex of death itself. This is what he means when he cries, "out of the depths." We don't know how this happened or why, but we do know that he feels close to the grave. In other words, the psalmist understands suffering.

While teetering on the edge of the abyss, the psalmist has a choice: he can mourn his fretful condition or he can cry out to the Lord. Of course, as both our voice and our guide, he leads us in crying out.

Forgiveness of Sins

How will he be rescued? Will God subdue his enemies? Will he bring healing? The psalmist needs something powerful and he needs it soon. He feels like his life is in the balance and, without deliverance, he has minutes left, not days.

Deliverance comes, but, as is God's custom, it comes in a way we couldn't have predicted. To be honest, at first glance it seems like a lame rescue attempt. The psalmist is given what appears to be a flimsy lifeline: his God is the one who forgives sins.

This one takes some reflection. We don't have evidence that the psalmist's sin caused his suffering. How is he going to take hope in the fact that he is forgiven? How will that rescue him? It seems like a pat spiritual answer to a life or death predicament. If you heard that from a friend, you *might* say "thanks" but you certainly wouldn't turn in that direction for help again. On the hierarchy of needs, physical survival seems more basic than spiritual encouragement. But the psalmist is clear on this. He is, without apology, presenting forgiveness of sins as the deepest answer of all. From his perspective, with forgiveness of sins he has hit the mother lode.

To appreciate the psalm's guidance on this, we have to believe that sin is a problem in our lives. In fact, to really be led by the psalm, we must realize that sin is our deepest problem, even deeper than our depression. Robert Fleming, a persecuted Scottish minister who lived from 1630-1694, said, "In the worst of times, there is still more cause to complain of an evil heart than of an evil world." In a culture where sin is not part of our normal public discourse, to adopt such a perspective will take some work.

Here are some questions to help you get started.

Do you believe that seeing sin in yourself is a good thing? Here you are, feeling like your self-worth couldn't be lower, and the discussion turns to sin. Why not just pound the final nail into the coffin? But, contrary to popular opinion, sin is a good thing. More specifically, when we see sin in ourselves it is a good thing. It is good on two counts. First, sin might feel natural but we were originally created to live without it. True humanness – blessed humanness – is sinless humanness. Of course, on this side of heaven perfection is impossible, but as we battle with sin we get tastes of how we were intended to live.

Second, when we see sin, it is evidence that God is close. It is the Holy Spirit who reveals sin (John 16:8). We don't have the acumen for it. If you see it, have hope – the Holy Spirit is at work in your life. It is tangible evidence of God's love.

Do you believe that sin is against God? To go one step further, while it may be easy to acknowledge that you sin – who doesn't? – it is tougher to acknowledge that your sin is against God.

We don't think of most wrongdoing as personal. If we break a law, we are not thinking that we violated city council, Congress or whatever body made the law. But biblical law-breaking is much more personal. It is more like adultery than speeding. Adulterers may feel like they are just doing what they want, but when they are exposed, they realize that their wrongdoing was highly personal. Yes, they are doing what they want, but they are also doing it *against* the spouse. In a similar way, we don't always realize that sin is conscious rebellion against God. We don't immediately see that every command arises out of God's character, and each violation dishonors him. The entire process is much more covert. Only when the Holy Spirit shines his light on our hearts do we realize that sin is personal.

Do you believe that sin is found in imaginations, motives, thoughts, and deeds? Although we may go through a day without other people actually seeing our sin, we can't go through an hour without sinning at the level of our thoughts and imaginations. It is there, at the level of the human heart, that you will find selfishness, pride, a desire to be loved rather than love, anger and lack of forgiveness, jealousy, complaining, grumbling, and thanklessness to the God who forgives. All these might be hidden from everyone else, but they are apparent to God.

Can you pinpoint, right now, a handful of sins? Now for the acid test: What sins do you see right now in your own life? Don't list ways you have not always succeeded in life; list ways you *presently* sin against God. Start with the obvious ones: you don't love deeply from the heart; you are concerned with your own success more than God and his kingdom; you are prideful and stand in judgment of others. Then you can get more specific. If you fail on this one, the psalm is meaningless.

The psalmist knew that his sin problem was deeper and more critical than his suffering. (And remember that, if he authored biblical psalms, he was a decent, fairly moral guy. If *he* knows his sin, we should too.) He also knew that no other god forgave such infractions without interminable penance. But his God, the triune God of Scripture, did not keep a record of wrongs for all those who turned to him. Therefore, the psalmist stood in awe. He could not comprehend such love, but he was thankful for it.

Exactly how God could forgive rebellion is unclear in the psalm. We, however, know how God could do such a thing. The psalmist anticipates the cross of Christ where God himself bore the just penalty for the rebellion of his creatures.

> Very rarely will anyone die for a righteous man, though for a good man someone might possibly dare to die. But God demonstrates his love for us in this: While we were still sinners, Christ died for us. (Rom. 5:7)

Such insight would have left the psalmist speechless.

Hope

Love produces hope. If we, in our misery, are absolutely persuaded of God's love, we will be confident that he will deliver us. Therefore, we hope in him. We can wait as long as it takes, because we are sure that he hears us and loves us. He *will* come. He *will* deliver. In fact, he is on the move right now. God's love inspires both an eagerness to be with him and a confidence that he is true to his word, so we know he will come. It is these two – eagerness and confidence – that combine to form hope.

When love is involved, time moves at a different pace. When Jacob served seven years for his wife-to-be Rachel, "they seemed like only a few days to him because of his love for her" (Gen. 29:20). Contrast this with what feels like the never-ending present-tense of suffering with depression: relief will never come, sleep will never come, the morning will never come.

The reality is that we are the watchmen on the last watch of the night. It is 4:30 a.m. We have seen the sunrise many times, and we are eager for it and confident it will come. What is the sunrise we are waiting for? In Psalm 130, the morning sun is a person. In that person are many benefits such as healing, deliverance, and love, but, make no mistake, it is a person. We wait for *him* more than for his gifts. We are not like children who eagerly wait to get to Grandmom's because she will have presents. We are like married lovers whose spouse is soon to return after a long trip. Just seeing the person is enough, whether he or she bears gifts or not.

Be careful at this point that you aren't discouraged by the psalmist. His enthusiasm is inspiring, but difficult to match. If it isn't quite contagious, don't despair. To move from the depths to a confident hope takes practice. Consider this psalm a condensed version of a long learning process.

God has determined that many good things come through perseverance. Look around and see how you have had to keep working at something before you learned it. Sports, hobbies, vocations, even relationships – they all follow the same pattern. So don't expect hope to happen immediately. It would be like insisting that you play Mozart before your second piano lesson. Hope is both a gift from God and a skill he enables us to attain. The point is that you *can* have the psalmist's hope.

Encouraging Others

When you receive something wonderful, you talk about it. The news can't be contained. In this psalm, what began as the cry of an isolated man becomes a shout to the community. "If I have found hope and love in the Lord, then you can too. If I have found joy in forgiveness, you can too." Or, to paraphrase,

"If I, an Old Testament psalmist who hasn't seen the coming of Jesus, can speak with this kind of hope, how much more can you, who have witnessed the cross – the unmistakable evidence of forgiveness of sins?"

Granted, this may still seem like an impossible dream, but remember that God himself is giving you this psalm. He is rewriting your story. You might feel like you are doing very well to repeat the cries of the first two verses, but the Spirit of God wants you to have the entire story.

This is just one psalm of many you could own. It can belong to you and be your future. Think about it. You feel like you have no purpose. Think of what it would be like to be an ambassador of hope to hopeless people. Those who have struggled with depression are especially credible because of their suffering; their hope is tried and genuine. When *you* speak hope to another, it is persuasive and attractive.

Response

Sometimes you have to force-feed yourself. You aren't hungry. You don't want to eat. But you know you must. Now is a time to force-feed. Your spiritual health depends on it.

You are not accustomed to doing something without *feeling* like doing it. If you have tried it, no doubt it feels odd and mechanical. It does not feel very human, because we are so accustomed to being mobilized by our passion. But be assured that this is *very* human. When animals have instincts – their version of feelings – they are slaves to them. You, however, can override your instincts. You can act out of wisdom and faith.

If this psalm suits you, stick with it. Highlight it, re-read it, speak about it. It will take practice to make it your own.

What is your plan for remembering?

CHAPTER 9

Purpose

Too often we live on little scraps of meaning. It is amazing how we can survive on so little: a three-percent raise, a new pair of shoes, a one-night stand, an internet relationship. We manage to eke out meaning and purpose from fumes. That is, of course, until you submerge into depression. Then you notice that there is no larger story, and the stage collapses.

> There come moments when our work – that activity by which we discover our worth in the world – there come moments, I say, when our profession, our daily labor, suddenly looks like a painted set in a theater, and the set collapses. All our valuable work collapses, and with horror we stare to the other side of material things, the spiritual deeps where we always believed meaning to be, but we see nothing. Bare nothing.[1]

Depression feels like a state of not-thinking, but it is also a

---

[1] A. Camus, *The Myth of Sisyphus* (New York: Vintage, 1955), p. 10.

place of insight because you see that the stage was really just a stage. What seemed meaningful and real a few years ago has turned out to be a façade. Pleasures were fleeting. Nothing lasted. Marriage became stale.

Such insight, of course, is painful, and it feels like it could cost you your life. But if you are willing, the next step begins a significant stretch on the path of wisdom. Many sages have traveled this way.

> "Meaningless! Meaningless!" says the Teacher.
> "Utterly meaningless! Everything is meaningless."
> What does man gain from all his labor at which he
> toils under the sun? (Eccl. 1:1-2)

This, however, is the way he starts, not the way he finishes.

Depression says, "You will not find meaning in what you are doing," and depression is right. What it doesn't tell you is, "Keep looking, you will find it. You are a creature with a royal purpose." For this, you need to listen to others who have gone this way before. They urge you to continue and point the way.

Fear God and Keep His Commandments

When you observe life and listen to wise people, you will quickly find that *it is not about us*, which hurts our pride but is a welcome relief. We simply can't invest our hopes, dreams and love in the self because it was never intended to carry such freight. For that matter, there is *nothing* created that was intended to sustain such hopes. Creation is to be enjoyed, but we don't put our trust in it. The only alternative is God himself.

The Teacher in the book of Ecclesiastes tries to save us time in our search for meaning and purpose. He tells us that he tried to make life about himself and it didn't work. He tried learning, laughter, great projects, unbridled sexual pleasure, money, music and children. None of them, when they were elevated to his life's purpose, led to anything but despair. He could not find his purpose in the created world.

After briefly envying an ordinary life of honest toil, good friends, food, moderate drink and doing right, he comes to his answer – his purpose.

> Now all has been heard; here is the conclusion of the matter: Fear God and keep his commandments, for this is the whole duty of man. (Eccl. 12:13)

Don't be put off by the word "fear" in "fear God." It is a more expansive word in Scripture than our idea of being afraid of someone. It includes awe, honor, reverence, and worship. And, yes, there is a certain way that it is appropriate to fear God, but not because of potential condemnation. If you have put your trust in Christ, condemnation will not fall on you. We fear God because he is God. He is not tame and domesticated like we sometimes make him out to be.

The fear of God is how we respond to the fact that God is greater than we are – different from us – in all things. His beauty is greater. His wisdom is greater. His love is greater. And, yes, his anger is greater. Simply put, he is God and we are not.

In an era when it is stylish to soften the character of God, "fear" is a wonderful antidote. There are times when, knowing who God is and what he has done, our knees should be knocking. Martin Luther, for example, was persuaded that we should be terror-stricken by the sufferings of Christ, because those sufferings reveal that our sin is so serious and deserves such serious judgment. Of course, he didn't stop there. He also was persuaded that we should be trembling at the knowledge of

God's love, which is greater than anything we have ever known or given.[2]

Fearing God and keeping his commandments brings a certain simplicity to life. He is the Creator, we are the creatures. We belong to him. When he directs us, we follow. We come before him and say, "And how do you want me to live today?" The psalmist goes so far as to say that his affliction was valuable because it taught him more about keeping God's commandments, which was his delight (Ps. 119:71).

There are, of course, many commands to be found in Scripture. No one can keep them all in mind. But we can easily remember the summary of God's law: love one another. What does that have to do with purpose and meaning? Every command in Scripture is a purpose statement. We are servants of the exalted king. When he speaks to us and tells us what to do, that becomes our purpose. Our purpose is to live for his purposes.

Sadly, this doesn't enthuse many of us. It is too simple, and we are too American to think that serving someone above us can be a good thing. We think that living for our purposes is more satisfying. But you know better. Ecclesiastes makes sense to you. You have tried other purposes and they were found wanting. You have also been forewarned that we are on terrain where spiritual warfare rages, so you have to walk very carefully. We can be easily deceived about those things that are most important.

Stop and think. A very wise person, the writer of Ecclesiastes, has just summarized your purpose. He knows that this purpose is the path of life. He knows what the heart really wants. He is pleading with you to listen to his conclusion and adopt it as your own.

---

[2] S. Nichols, *Martin Luther: A Guided Tour of his Life and Thought* (Phillipsburg, N.J.: P & R, 2002).

Be willing to try it. How can you keep God's commands today? Look for someone to love. A wise older counselor, who had experienced depression himself, challenged other depressed people this way: "Fight the spiritual battles that accompany depression so that you can love other people." It sounds simple, but it is the summary of many years of experience.

Love God and Love Neighbor, and Other Purpose Statements

If you are familiar with Scripture, you will find the summary of Ecclesiastes in a number of different forms.

> And what does the LORD require of you? To act justly and to love mercy and to walk humbly with your God. (Mic. 6:8)

> Love the Lord your God with all your heart and with all your soul and with all your mind. This is the first and greatest commandment. And the second is like it: Love your neighbor as yourself. (Matt. 22:37-39)

> The only thing that counts is faith expressing itself through love. (Gal. 5:6)

The language varies: fear the Lord, trust him, love him, walk humbly with him, or believe in him. Then we express this commitment to the Lord by obeying his commandments, the summary of which is love. This is the true foundation for human life. Apart from it, life is meaningless.

Stop again. Consider how you are responding. Does this sound superficial? Stale? Pie-in-the-sky? Too easy? Important, but you can't seem to work up any enthusiasm for it? Reflect on this one. Talk it out with another person. Don't think that you have already tried it and it didn't work. If you think that this is passé or irrelevant, you are revealing your purpose: to be rid of depression. That, of course, is worthwhile, but don't elevate it to your purpose in life.

If in doubt, assume that your purpose is not in synch with God's. You have most likely "tried" this purpose much less than you think. Although you might intellectually know your purpose, aspiring to it is very different, and living it out is more different still. The reality is that no one wholeheartedly aspires to it; no one consistently lives out of it. So begin with confession. Tell your Heavenly Father that you are like a prodigal child who keeps looking for self-oriented purposes rather than God-oriented ones.

There is another reality too. You can grow, day to day, with the Spirit of God energizing you, making this more and more of the purpose of your life. As you do, you will be changed.

Glorify God

Since Scripture has so much to say about our purpose, it has a rich vocabulary for it. One particularly fine word is the word *glorify*. We are created to glorify God. In the book of Ephesians, Paul reminds us three times in his introduction that we live "to the praise of his glory" (Eph. 1:6, 12, 14).

When we think of glory, we think of something big, beautiful, and obvious. "What a glorious sunset this evening!" "Her aria was simply glorious." To glorify God means to have our lives make him obvious and beautiful. We want him to be famous. We want to draw attention to the glorious God who loved us, and we do that by trusting him and loving others.

In 1646 over one hundred clergymen met, at the request of the English king, to develop a summary of biblical teaching that would be suitable to guide the church. In the children's catechism they developed (which is a series of questions and answers), the first question had to do with our purpose:

What is the chief end of man? Man's chief end is to glorify God and enjoy him forever.[3]

They are right. This is our purpose. It is not about us; it is about God and his purposes. What could be bigger and grander than that? This is no little scrap of meaning.

Christ Crucified

To test the quality of the purpose statement you choose, examine the place of Jesus Christ in it. Our response of fear, love, praise and worship comes from the knowledge of him. We glorify God because of what Jesus has done.

When you page through Scripture with an eye to finding purpose statements, you can't miss the apostle Paul's summary because he says it is "of first importance."

> For what I received I passed on to you as of first importance: that Christ died for our sins according to the Scriptures, that he was buried, that he was raised on the third day according to the Scriptures, and that he appeared to Peter, and then to the Twelve. After that he appeared to more than five hundred of the brothers at the same time. (1 Cor. 15:3-6)

If you want an even more basic statement, Paul whittles it down to this: "Christ and him crucified" (1 Cor. 2:2). When he personalizes it, he writes, "For to me, to live is Christ and to die is gain" (Phil. 1:21). Scripture is a story that climaxes in Christ. Our story, if it is to have enduring purpose, must stay focused

---

[3] The Westminster Shorter Catechism (available at various web sites).

on that same conclusion.

What's the use? Why bother? The answer is that Jesus Christ has been crucified and he has risen from the dead. You couldn't find a more complete answer. In it you find that you are called, forgiven, adopted into a new family, given gifts, given a mission, given a future. You are given love, and this love is so extreme it will take you all eternity to begin to understand it.

Put it this way: at the cross, Christ has taken your story of misery upon himself and he has given you his story of resurrection and hope. We are given the successes of Christ, the record of Christ, and the love that Jesus enjoys from the Father. When you put your faith in Jesus, everything changes. What some people think is just a ticket into heaven is much, much more. There are future *and* present benefits to the blood of Jesus. Through faith, you are brought into the royal family with all its rights and privileges. At first, you might feel like a stranger who doesn't belong, but when the Father keeps assuring you that the cross of Christ delivered your adoption papers, you eventually begin to look around the palace corridors and say that the pictures on the walls are *your* relatives. Instead of asking for an audience with the king, you will say that God is *your* God (Ps. 63:1) and *your* Father (Matt. 6:9).

Bearing a Family Resemblance

Fear God and keep his commandments, love God and others, glorify God, "for me to live is Christ" – these are all purpose statements. They are all different ways of reminding us who we really are. Human beings were created as God's royal offspring, intended to bear the distinct character of the Father. Our purpose is to bear a family resemblance. What God's law does is describe the character of the King so we can imitate him.

But there are prodigal yearnings within each of us. We want

to find our own way. Even though we get hopelessly lost, there is something in us that prefers aimless wandering to child-like imitation and obedience. The cross is God's pursuit of wayward children. It is the invitation back to the family.

"Be holy, because I am holy" (Lev. 11:44, 19:2, 20:8, 20:26), "be imitators of God" (Eph. 5:1), "live as children of light" (Eph. 5:8), "your attitude should be the same as that of Christ Jesus" (Phil. 2:5) – these are familial exhortations. Study Jesus, your older brother and your God, and imitate him by faith. This is our purpose.

> God disciplines us for our good, that we *may share in his holiness....* It produces a harvest of righteousness and peace for those who have been trained by it. (Heb. 12:10-11)

One verse in Scripture that has been hastily pinned on all suffering is Romans 8:28: "And we know that in all things God works for the good of those who love him, who have been called according to his purpose." How can your suffering be good in any way? The answer comes in the next verse. The good is that we are being "conformed to the likeness of his Son." This is what we are intended to be. This is our purpose, and as you are more and more aligned with your purpose, your experience of depression will change.

Timothy Richard in his book, *Forty-Five Years in China* (1916), wrote about a Chinese cult leader trying to accuse Christians. As evidence against them, he held up a surgical text used by some of the missionary doctors. "Ignorant of the humane objective of surgery, he regarded operations as proof of the cruelty of Christians." Suffering is God's surgery that leads to health when responded to by faith.

Chapter Nine

Response

Do you want to see evidence of the Holy Spirit in your life? When you say, "Why bother?" answer, "Because of Jesus." Many times our lives intersect nicely with God's laws because his laws make sense. Life tends to go better when we speak the truth, forgive, love, and don't murder. But sometimes our desires and God's seem out of synch. We want to go one way and God calls us to another. Or we feel paralyzed when God calls us to act. It is at those times that faith and the work of the Holy Spirit will be apparent.

C. S. Lewis makes this observation in an imaginary dialogue between two demons.

> [Screwtape warns Wormwood] Our cause is never more in danger than when a human, no longer desiring, but still intending, to do our Enemy's [God's] will, looks around upon a universe from which every trace of Him seems to have vanished, and asks why he has been forsaken, and still obeys.[4]

What will imitation or obedience look like? Since Jesus became a man, thereby giving great dignity to the ordinary activities of human life, we should expect that purpose-driven faith will look fairly ordinary. For some, it will mean "do the next thing." Put one step in front of the other. It will look like serving God and others by greeting them, asking about them, praying for them. It will be saying, "Lord, I am willing, what would you have me do today?"

What is your purpose?

---

[4] C. S. Lewis, *The Screwtape Letters* (New York: Macmillan, 1977), p. 39.

CHAPTER 10

Persevere

Depression says, "Surrender." The message is relentless, and many comply, because even when you know that there is a purpose to your suffering, the battle seems too long. "I can't tell you how tired I am of character building experiences," says an author who has been through it a number of times.[1] If depression's assault only touched one part of your life, you might put up a fight. But when it gains access to every sector, and even the smallest step is oppressive, "surrender" seems inevitable. You can postpone it but not avoid it.

In Scripture, the word "surrender" links you directly to "persevere, be patient in trials." This doesn't sound very liberating, to be sure. "Hang in there," "keep at it," "you can do it" are trite and unhelpful responses when offered by friends and family. It's as if they have nothing else to say, so they offer this "encouragement" just to say something.

The call to persevere may not sound any more appealing

---

[1] Kay Jamison, cited by A. Solomon, "Anatomy of Melancholy," *The New Yorker*, January 12, 1998, p. 61.

when it comes from God himself. It *does* sound more authoritative. It sounds like a general telling his troops to keep going in the face of a much stronger enemy. But it can still sound hollow.

But remember once again that we cannot avoid God. All paths lead to him. If you are tempted to skip over his words on perseverance, remember that he is life. His words give life. Whatever he says is surprising in its beauty and elegance, and is of invaluable worth. In other words, there is more to perseverance than you think.

God Perseveres

As with so many commands of Scripture, "persevere" is more than something God says; it is something he does. It is one of the many aspects of his character. The reason it is of great worth is that it is one of the chief ways God has revealed himself to us. Scripture consistently points to God's perseverance and forbearance with his people.

> The Lord is not slow in keeping his promise, as some understand slowness. He is *patient* with you, not wanting anyone to perish, but everyone to come to repentance. (2 Peter 3:9)

> For I *endure* scorn for your sake, and shame covers my face. (Ps. 69:7)

> May the Lord direct your hearts into God's love and Christ's *perseverance*. (2 Thess. 3:5)

> Let us fix our eyes on Jesus, the author and perfecter of our faith, who for the joy set before him *endured*

the cross, scorning its shame, and sat down at the right hand of the throne of God. (Heb. 12:2)

Perseverance is only relevant in difficulties, and we are, in fact, very difficult people for God to deal with. Our Creator God has created us for himself and we respond too often with indifference or a quest for adolescent independence. Put even more personally, we are his beloved, but, in the face of God's unexplainable and lavish love, we pursue other lovers who ultimately abandon us. In this context, God reveals his perseverance with us.

"How can I give you up? How can I hand you over? My heart is changed within me; all my compassion is aroused. I will not carry out my fierce anger. For I am God, and not man – the Holy One among you. I will not come in wrath. When the Lord roars like a lion, his children will return." (Hos. 11:8-10, author's paraphrase)

The apostle Paul highlighted this patience and perseverance. As one who persecuted the followers of Jesus, even overseeing their deaths, Paul was the last person in the world you would expect God to use as his most influential missionary.

But for that very reason I was shown mercy so that in me, the worst of sinners, Christ Jesus might display his unlimited *patience* as an example for those who would believe on him and receive eternal life. (1 Tim. 1:16)

All teaching on perseverance, patience, and endurance finds

its source in the character of God. Just as we love because he is love and he loved us before we knew him, so we persevere because he is perseverance and he has persevered with us throughout history.

Perseverance in Everyday Life

If you farm or do gardening, you know something about perseverance. When you plant seeds, the ground will not yield corn quickly. When you plant fruit trees and grapevines, it could be a few years before you actually eat their fruit.

When you decide to take up the violin, the instrument produces squeaks and scratchings long before it reluctantly yields Beethoven etudes. If you have skill in anything at all, it has come through persevering.

Children are notoriously poor at waiting and persevering.

"When will we get to Grandmom's house?"

"Soon," is the typical though unsatisfying reply.

"Mommy, when you are going to play with me?"

"Not yet. Not until I finish this report." Fifteen seconds later the child asks the same question, this time with a tone of voice that can drive you mad.

But the child is in us all. We too look forward to the day when we have learned perseverance before the Lord. It is the older wise man or woman who can take the many hassles of life in stride, without grumbling and complaining, with contentment rather than resignation.

God has chosen to inject his character of perseverance and patient waiting into everyday, earthly life. We are patiently waiting for the Lord's coming. Creation itself is patiently waiting for the time when it will be liberated from bondage (Rom. 8:22).

Be *patient*, then, brothers, until the Lord's coming. See

how the farmer waits for the land to yield its valuable crop and how patient he is for the autumn and spring rains. (James 5:7)

God could have ushered in the end times immediately after Jesus ascended into heaven, but, for various reasons, he has chosen to wait patiently.

Perseverance in Suffering

Although opportunities to grow in perseverance are available every day, suffering is what makes perseverance a necessary skill.

Not only so, but we also rejoice in our sufferings, because we know that suffering produces *perseverance*. (Rom. 5:3)

Therefore, since we are surrounded by such a great cloud of witnesses [who have gone through suffering] let us throw off everything that hinders and the sin that so easily entangles, and let us run with *perseverance* the race marked out for us. (Heb. 12:1)

The testing of your faith develops *perseverance*. (James 1:3)

As you know, *we consider blessed those who have persevered.* You have heard of Job's *perseverance* and have seen what the Lord finally brought about. The Lord is full of compassion and mercy. (James 5:11)

Make every effort to add to your faith goodness; and to goodness, knowledge; and to knowledge, self-

> control; and to self-control, *perseverance*; and to *perseverance*, godliness. (2 Peter 1:5-6)

If Jesus Christ learned obedience and endurance through what he suffered, why would we expect our lives to be different? Through our struggles and pain, we are being offered perseverance, the character of God. Hardships are intended to give us a spiritual makeover, "that we may share in his holiness" (Heb. 12:10). Therefore, when God encourages us to persevere, he is not stumbling for encouraging words. He is teaching us how to look like him.

Given this connection to the character of God, perseverance is not ordinary but glorious. Think about it for a moment. Let's say you just heard a testimony from someone who said she had been depressed until God completely delivered her. She is, of course, ecstatic. But could it be that she was putting her trust in being healed rather than in the God who loves, forgives, perseveres and heals?

Now consider another woman who has experienced deep depression. Her testimony is that she believes God is good, whether depression leaves or returns. She has learned to persevere in troubles and find contentment in God in the midst of them. *That* is a glorious testimony.

Perseverance isn't flashy. It doesn't call attention to itself. It looks like putting one foot in front of another. But beneath the surface, where few can see the glory, is something very profound (Rev. 2:2,19). You are becoming more like God. God sees it and he is pleased by it.

Perseverance is more than just making it through life until you die from natural causes. It is perseverance in faith and obedience. It is perseverance in our God-given purpose, even when life is very hard. Perseverance asks the question, "Today, how will I represent God? How will I trust him and follow him in obedience?" Then it asks for help from others, cries out to the Lord, and looks for an opportunity to love. It may seem feeble, but our confidence is in the God who is strong. The essence of persevering is trusting or obeying *because of Jesus.*

Perseverance in Battle

What you thought was a *path* of life now looks more like a battlefield. Satan's strategy is to wear you down. You remember the cross one day and Satan is content to wait for tomorrow. If he can't outfight you (because God fights for you), he tries to outwait you. Perseverance is what you need in prolonged wars.

Paul says to Timothy, "Endure hardship with us like a good soldier of Christ Jesus" (2 Tim. 2:3). Martin Luther called depression *anfechtungen*, which means "to be fought at." What a perfect name! Instead of being translated as "something to surrender to," it is a call to arms. Martyn Lloyd-Jones, the British pastor-physician who thought deeply about depression, addresses the topic in a Pattonesque speech. Hear him, however, as a physician of the soul who wants the very best for those who listen.

> You have to take yourself in hand . . . You must turn on yourself, upbraid yourself, condemn yourself, exhort yourself, and say to yourself, "Hope thou in God" – instead of muttering in this depressed, unhappy way.[2]

Wise counsel tells us that we must talk to depression – fight it – rather than merely listen to it. What we often hear from

---

[2] Martyn Lloyd-Jones, *Spiritual Depression* (Grand Rapids: Eerdmans, 1990), p.21.

depression is, "God doesn't care" – if, indeed, we hear God's name at all. What we say to it is, "Put your hope in God."

> Why are you downcast, O my soul?
>> Why so disturbed within me?
> Put your hope in God,
>> for I will yet praise him,
>> my Savior and my God. (Ps. 42:5-6,11)

"Hope." There it is again. Hope is the constant companion of perseverance.

In the midst of prolonged battles, commanders offer words of encouragement and hope, words like:

> You are the best fighting unit in the world. The battle in front of us will be difficult, and there will be casualties, but you will win. And don't forget why you are here. You have a purpose – a duty. You are fighting for democracy and freedom. You are fighting for your country.

By giving them hope, the goal is to rouse the troops to persevere. God's Word gives you daily encouragement. In fact, all Scripture is his means of sustaining you in the battle.

> For everything that was written in the past was written to teach us, so that through *endurance* and the encouragement of the Scriptures we might have hope. (Rom. 15:4)

Your hope is that God hears, that he finds great worth in perseverance, that he rewards those who seek him (Heb. 11:6), that he blesses those who persevere (James 1:12), that he is faithful to all his promises. Your hope comes when you begin to fix your eyes on Jesus, the One who is invisible (Heb. 11:27).

Sound impossible? If you cannot be aroused to hope, you are in good company. There was a point in Job's life when he said, "What strength do I have, that I should still hope? What prospects, that I should be patient?" (Job 6:11). But even in his despair, Job continued to seek his God. So, at least, seek him.

If even that seems too much, ride on someone else's hope for as long as you need. Consider Abraham, Moses, Joseph, and many others who knew that God had something better planned (Heb. 11). Let your friends or family read Scripture to you. Let them tell you about their hope and confidence in Christ.

There are many different ways of doing battle. Call out to the persevering God who gives endurance (Rom. 15:5). He will answer you.

Response

Here is a map that assembles some of the pieces of perseverance (Figure 10.1). It starts with you reciting, "You, O God, are strong, and… you, O Lord, are loving" (Ps. 62:12). Or, you listen as God says to you, "I love you and I am the Mighty God." From there it travels to hope and purpose, which lead us to perseverance. It doesn't stop, however, at perseverance. Perseverance and patient endurance find grace from God, which gives us deeper knowledge of his love and sovereign strength. This in turn leads to a greater sense of purpose and greater confidence in God, which sends us toward a new place of perseverance.

Figure 10.1. A Map for Perseverance.

If you feel unable to persevere, you may be skipping some of the steps needed to get there. So review who God is, and be able to articulate your purpose and your hope. If perseverance still seems elusive, you might want to consider how you already have received it. For example, are you in any way open to what has been written so far? That is evidence of perseverance, and it is more beautiful than you think. God is greatly pleased by it. If you need more evidence, ask a friend if he or she sees any evidence of perseverance in you.

Still can't fight? Remember that God gives you other people so that you do not fight alone. When you feel thoroughly exhausted, call for help. The church functions like a tag-team wrestling match. Just get to the ropes and touch the other person's hand. Their perseverance can carry you.

PART TWO *Listening to Depression*

CHAPTER 11

Depression Has Its Reasons: Other People, "Adam," and Satan

Now listen more carefully to depression. Like all feelings, it is a kind of language.

Guilt says, "I am wrong."

Anger says, "You are wrong."

Fear says, "I am in danger."

Depression, too, has a message, but the message is usually not that simple. Whereas some emotions are clear and unambiguous, depression's language is more heavily encrypted. It might take some decoding before it is understandable, but it is worth the effort.

Reconstructing the History of Depression

Emotions have a history. To put a complex process as simply as possible, their history consists of two parts: (1) events outside of us, which include physical problems, and (2) beliefs, spiritual allegiances, and interpretations within us. The interaction of these two, over time, is what causes depression (Figure 11.1).

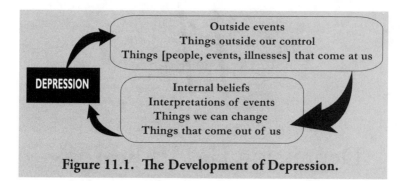

Figure 11.1. The Development of Depression.

Keeping this interaction in mind challenges us to investigate. Depression doesn't just appear out of nowhere. It has its reasons. And although we have already found that it isn't essential to know the reasons, we still look for them. For example, if your car stopped in the middle of nowhere and there was no phone available, God would certainly give you grace to live by faith in the midst of that hardship. This does not mean, however, that you wouldn't look under the hood. Even if you knew nothing about cars, you would do the standard wire-wiggling and engine-staring.

With depression, God gives grace to live in the midst of hardships. He also gives grace to investigate it more carefully.

Start with outside events. Even though the connection between certain events and the feelings of depression might have faded over the years, depression can often point to something or someone – a divorce, a serious accident, or an abusive past, to name a few. Perhaps one event can't accept all the responsibility, but it can still be significant because it was either first or most intense. It provoked an approach to life that eventually, sometimes only after many years, culminated in depression.

The basic categories for external events are other people, the general curse on creation that came through Adam, and Satan (see Chapter 4).

Other People

Other people are the easiest cause to identify. Whether through an abusive past or a recent rejection, other people bring the greatest pain into our lives. Although the connection is usually obvious, this cause can get harder to identify when the sins of others have become either so distant or so habitual that we don't recognize them as a serious offense.

Linda, now thirty-eight, said that her circumstances couldn't be better but her depression couldn't be worse. Her husband loves her, her children are healthy and growing in Christ, and she has enough money to pay bills with cash to spare at the end of each month. When she reviewed her past, it too seemed relatively smooth and uneventful. She was raised in a prosperous home, her parents were still together, and she was offered guidance by both her parents.

Her childhood home, Linda said, had been structured. There were clear guidelines and expectations, which made her feel "secure and loved." When asked for specifics, however, Linda recounted expectations that were inordinate and oppressive. Grades, future career, the resumé of each prospective spouse, clothes, all school decisions from elementary to graduate school – these were just a few of the areas her father controlled. Tears, apparent weakness, and independent choice were unacceptable. What was odd was that Linda appeared unaffected by all this, as if her past were good and normal.

When asked about her history of depression, she calmly summarized that she had been hospitalized in a psychiatric institution at age thirteen "because I was never hungry." She started taking psychiatric medication at that time and, except for pregnancies and times when psychiatrists changed prescriptions, she had been taking something ever since.

What would it be like to live in a world where mistakes, as defined by a father, were unacceptable? What would it be like to live in an environment that was controlled to the last detail? To this day, when authority figures speak, Linda seems to become glazed and subservient, never questioning, even when requests are ungodly.

Thus depression, in a strange way, suits her. She is numb, so she doesn't have to live with the sadness and regret. She feels like she can't think clearly, so outside authority isn't questioned. Every act of submission or doing the expected then contributes to a sense of depersonalization and loss of identity.

Making these connections was an important start for Linda. She began to see that what she was feeling was most likely linked, in some way, to the daily patterns of the home in which she was raised. Once she saw this, she was pointed to issues in her relationship with God. Her operative belief system embodied significant falsehoods.

When you partner with someone who is suffering, you will often find that people were part of the difficult circumstances. Pain is usually tied to something that happened to us. Does this matter any more? Does it matter to God? God's sovereign control over history and our own personal stories make past situations *more* important, not less. What happened to us was not a series of random, unrelated events.

Adam and the Curse on Creation

When Adam sinned, the creation that had been blessed and pronounced "very good" by God fell under judgment. Work suddenly became difficult, relationships had tensions, physical bodies were prone to disease and would waste away, and death cast its long shadow over everything. Even weather would no longer cooperate. Instead of a predictable mist watering a fertile garden, droughts, typhoons, tornados, floods and earthquakes would remind us that even the earth groans. Nothing in all creation is quite right.

Physical ill health. The decline of our physical bodies is one possible cause of depression. It may seem odd to locate this cause among other external circumstances in our lives, because the physical body *is* us. But we are more than our physical body, and the body has much in common with other external causes. Most prominently, external causes are largely out of our control. We don't always like them, but there is not always much we can do about them. In this sense, the body that is wasting away is another problem that comes at us – another circumstance of our lives.

Physical appearance, chronic disease, and chemical imbalances are a short list of significant physical contributions to depression.

Misery in work. Also included under the curse is the fact that labor seems futile and much more difficult since sin discolored the world. You spend years working on your house only to sell it and watch the next owner tear it down for something more contemporary. Enter data all day, but try not to think of how irrelevant it seems in the broad scheme of world events. With the curse, work has changed from a pleasure to a drudgery. Yes, there are times when God's original intent breaks through and we find satisfaction in our labor (even if it isn't going to change the course of history), but misery is never far away.

The perceived meaninglessness of work is often part of depression. It usually, however, is a sign of depression rather than a cause.

Death. The worst of the curse is death. You have lost loved ones, you will lose more, and they will lose you. There is no good death. If you lose someone to a sudden heart attack, you miss goodbyes and closure. If you lose someone whose chronic disease made death more predictable, you agonize with him as the disease changes him into someone he was not. Death, indeed, is a tireless enemy.

It's said that depression welcomes death, but it is not so much death that is welcomed as it is the alleviation of mental pain. Death itself is an enemy to everyone, and there is good reason to think that it contributes to the cause of depression even more than it is a result of it.

Isn't it true that death – especially when it isn't aggressively interpreted through the resurrection of Jesus Christ – *should* leave us depressed? Death renders everything meaningless. Why work? Why love? Why seek pleasure? It is fleeting. Death swallows everything. Its tides wash away every footprint we hope to leave.

Not that we are always thinking about it. Modern society has distanced us from death, and we do everything we can to avoid it. Physicians use a string of euphemisms, such as "passed away" and "resting peacefully." Comedians specialize in human frailties, but they won't touch death unless they quickly evoke images of angels and bliss. We might not consciously think about death, but be assured that, unless this enemy is dealt with head on, it leaves its mark on all earthly misery.

Age-defying lotions, the worship of youth and the marginalization of the aged, "free-floating anxiety," panic attacks, Type-A personality, boredom, the obsession with health, the status of physicians, purposelessness, hopelessness, and most fears – you will find death and the fear of death right below the surface.

Satan

Satan is another external cause of depression. We are already aware of the way his most vicious attacks question the power and love of God. But he does most of his work through strategic partnerships. Partnering with the curse, he apparently can affect weather (Job 1) and bring disease. Partnering with our own hearts, he causes oppression, murder, and inhumanity in its manifold form. *When* he partners is unclear. The curse on creation and our own tendency toward sin can affect us without his assistance, so there is really no way for us to know the precise percentages of who contributes what. That is why, when depression persists, we don't immediately say, "Satan did it."

Necessary, But Not Sufficient

Why is it that some people who experience these circumstances spiral into depression and others don't? It is because these circumstances do not cause depression by themselves. They are usually *necessary* to the depressive cycle, but they are not *sufficient* – that is, they can't make you depressed all on their own. These circumstances must also connect with an internal system of beliefs or an interpretive lens that will then plunge you down into depression. Even chemical imbalances need help if they are to become depression, especially a depression accompanied by hopelessness and self-accusations.

We all know people who have gone through the most tragic of circumstances and have remained hopeful. "We are hard pressed on every side, but not crushed; perplexed, but not in despair; persecuted, but not abandoned; struck down, but not destroyed" (2 Cor. 4:8-9). Some people avoid the deeper reaches of depression because they are constitutionally steady; others because their beliefs and confidence in God catch them before they fall too far.

111

Response

It is not especially encouraging to review the various contributors to your depression, but, if possible, generate a short list of the most obvious ones. It will remind you that depression usually comes from somewhere.

CHAPTER 12

Depression Has Its Reasons: Culture

There is no limit to the number of influences on depression. Scripture mentions the larger categories of other people, Satan, and the Adamic curse, and it gives many specifics, such as parents, teachers, peers, poor health, poverty, demons, and others. Yet the list is not intended to be exhaustive. Depressed people have suggested connections with the phases of the moon, stress in the womb, changes in the ozone layer, diet and exercise, and maybe they are right, in part. Some contributions, however, are more likely than others.

Over the past twenty years, those who study depression have observed that depression is on the increase. The incidence rate of depression for those born after 1950 is as much as twenty times higher than the incidence rate for those born before 1910.[1] Like all statistics, these can be molded to suit many different agendas, but it is a commonly accepted observation that depression has significantly increased over the last three generations. The question, of course, is why.

---

[1] James Buie, "'Me' Decades Generate Depression," *APA Monitor*, February 1991, p.18.

The most popular theory of depression today is the biochemical hypothesis, which suggests that depression is a consequence of serotonin deficiencies in the brain. No one, however, has succeeded in squaring this genetic hypothesis with the dramatic increase in the rate of depression. Instead, the best explanations point to some kind of cultural changes that have been shaped by us and seek to shape us in return.

Culture provides a way for us to see ourselves and the world. It emerges whenever people gather together. Therefore, families, schools, and church denominations all have particular cultures. Culture oversees the unwritten guidelines for manners, traditions, and relationships: whether or not we have dinner together, how we celebrate our holidays, whether we raise hands in worship or kneel, how we greet each other, and so on.

Infused through culture, however, is what Scripture refers to as the *world*. The world was created by God as the abode of human beings. As created by God it is good, but as our abode it bears the mark of our sin. Therefore, in the New Testament, the term *world* is used to denote the order of things that are alienated from God. In this sense, it is morally corrupt (2 Peter 1:4), peddling foolishness as wisdom (1 Cor. 1:20) and interpreting God's wisdom as foolishness (1 Cor. 1:23).

The world can be defined as the "corporate flesh,"[2] as if our sinful tendencies were singing in unison. As such, the world consists of patterns and structures that come from us. *We* are responsible, for example, for the unrestrained sensuality in our culture. But there is also a sense in which the world comes *at* us. Even though we don't need any assistance in sensual indulgence, the world plants the message that unbridled sensuality is good, thus abetting the tendencies of our own hearts.

---

[2] Richard Lovelace, *Renewal* (Downers Grove, Il: InterVarsity, 1985), p. 86.

Recognizing that the world is outside us heightens our awareness of the spiritual battle we must fight. Not only do we have to fight against our own sin, we also have to fight against aspects of the culture that applaud our sinful tendencies rather than rebuke them.

The following short list identifies features of our culture that have been linked with depression.

A Culture of Decisions

Martin Seligman, a world-renowned researcher on depression, has suggested this explanation for the increase in depression: "The modern individual is not the peasant of yore with a fixed future yawning ahead. He – and now she, effectively doubling the market – is a battleground of decisions and preferences."[3]

In previous generations, an implicit caste system kept us in the same jobs as our parents, and most of the major decisions in our lives were made before we were born. Your father was a blacksmith; you were a blacksmith. A boy in your village comes from the right family and his parents go to the right church; he is the one you will marry when you come of age. It was a system that had its problems, but the pressure of decisions was not one of them. Now, education, career, marriage, and even sexual preference are up for grabs. Life is a maelstrom of decisions.

And if the decisions don't get you, the pressure will. Parents reserve spots at select elementary schools soon after their children are born, hoping to give them any advantage possible in a highly competitive world. They try to provide every extracurricular experience humanly possible so children can find their strengths and, perhaps, be in a position for a college scholarship. Children feel the pressure to have vocational ideas by the time they enter

---

[3] Buie, p. 18.

ninth grade. Teenagers now make course decisions in high school that their parents did not have to make in college. And even preteens are exposed to sexual situations and their associated pressures and decisions.[4] Teens feel like they face weekly choices that could affect the entire course of their lives, and what if they make a poor choice? Although life before a sovereign God assures us that God is in control, accomplishing his good plans even through our poor choices, it is easy to lose sight of this reality. When we do, we can feel as if an unwise decision has forever doomed us to a path that is second best.

An understandable response to such a pressured culture is withdrawal, paralysis in the face of decisions, fear of making wrong ones, fatigue, and feeling like you could sleep for days and still be tired. In other words, depression is a fitting response to these cultural pressures. The reason it is important for friends and counselors to be alert to this possible cultural influence is that Scripture can now speak more meaningfully. For example, most depression check lists don't list "Do you understand the basics of decision making and the will of God?" But if this is part of the problem, friends can offer instruction in how to make wise decisions.[5] They can also remind you that, in view of God's sovereign control, God will accomplish his purposes in our lives even when we make decisions we later regret.

A Culture of the Individual

In 1984, Edward Scheiffelin studied a primitive tribe in New Guinea. Among his findings was an absence of despair, hopelessness, depression, or suicide. Studies among the Amish

---

[4] David Elkind describes these sociological changes in an old but still very relevant book, *The Hurried Child: Growing Up Too Fast Too Soon* (Reading MA: Addison Wesley Longman, Inc. 1989).

[5] E.g., James Petty, *Step By Step* (Phillipsburg, NJ: P&R, 1999).

have found similar results. What is similar in these two cultures is the way individuals are part of a larger community. While Western culture is a pseudo-community in which we occasionally cluster in like-minded groups, these cultures have extended families of different people with different interests who learn how to live and work together.

Think about it: how would the statistics on depression change if people felt they were part of a community? Part of a family? In modern Western culture there is nothing bigger than ourselves. Satisfaction doesn't come from serving others in our extended circle of relationships. Instead, we think it comes from consuming and gratifying personal needs. If a relationship doesn't suit our desires, it is expendable; we can move on to another. "How do I feel?" is the national obsession.

This exaltation of the individual is a cultural value that is gradually changing. There have been a number of Christian and secular critiques of the "me decades" lifestyle. The problem, however, is twofold. First, the damage has been done. The aloneness, isolation, and powerlessness of a self-driven life have already taken root. Second, in a mobile society that lacks spiritual empowerment to love and reconcile, there isn't much hope for something better.

If this feature of the world contributes to depression, our response is first to know the enthroned God. When we go into the courtroom of the King of Kings, we are in awe of him more than we are aware of ourselves. Our troubles become much smaller in contrast to his beauty and holiness. Then, when we listen to the King, his command to us is simple: love others as you have been loved. Love breaks the hold of individualism; it builds new communities out of the ashes of broken and fragmented relationships.

Finally, we band together in churches. Depressed people

avoid people and church commitments, but they can also complain about abject isolation. The answer is to humbly accept your purpose. "Let us not give up meeting together, as some are in the habit of doing, but let us encourage one another – and all the more as you see the Day approaching" (Heb. 10:25). Churches are not perfect. How could they be when we are the church? But the Spirit is with the gathering of his people. Church is where you will know more of God's grace.

A Culture of Self-Indulgence

A corollary to the culture of the individual is the culture of self-indulgence. Whether you look at past slogans of popular culture, such as "If it feels good, do it," popular psychology's "Follow your feelings," or the advertising that fuels our economy, we are surrounded by the belief that we can find something outside ourselves to fill or satisfy us.

The myth is that "one more" will finally bring satisfaction. The reality, of course, is that it just leaves us with a desire for two more, and then three, because we find that one didn't satisfy. A law of diminishing returns is always at work when our appetites run amok. For those with stamina, the cycle of craving and indulgence can go on for years, but many people glimpse the vanity of these pursuits before they are ruined by them. These are the people who might be prone to depression. Some of them just intuitively see through the promises of self-indulgence. Others have deprived themselves of nothing or reached the zenith of their careers and found it empty.

When we think about the things that can satisfy our lusts, we tend to think of things that satisfy physical desires, like drugs, food, and sex. But self-indulgence can also feed more psychological appetites. The most common desire has been called the need for self-esteem, the endless quest to feel good about ourselves. Some students of depression suggest that the increase in depression is due in part to the backlash of the self-esteem teaching.

The reasoning is straightforward. What happens when people are raised on a steady diet of "You are great, you can do anything, you deserve it, you are the best, you can get what you want"? Sooner or later they find that they are *not* great, they *can't* do everything, they are *not* the best, and they *can't* control it all. Depression and denial are the only two options left.

A Culture Where Happiness Is the Greatest Good

Ask those living in Western culture what they desire and you will begin to hear "happiness." Look through the senior pictures in a high school yearbook and the frequent ambition is "I want to be happy." Even Aristotle's *Ethics* suggests that happiness is the greatest good. Given such a goal, it is not surprising that we have an ambivalent relationship with hardship.

People who have experienced war have learned to accept the trials and sufferings of life. Among many wise, older citizens in American society, there is no desperate flight from suffering. Instead, there is a recognition that it is a part of life that can have some benefit. Yet among those in the post-World War II generation, a wisp of happiness is the goal, and suffering must be avoided at all costs. If there are hardships in a relationship, end it. If there is an unpleasant emotion, medicate it. It is a generation that perceives no value to any hardship. Like a pampered child who never experienced the regular storms of life, we lack the skill of growing through our trials.

I'm not suggesting that we should pursue hardships. When the pain can be lightened, it is usually a good thing to do. But the point is that we live in a culture that idolizes happiness, and if we idolize happiness, it will always elude us.

A Culture of Entertainment and Boredom

Another feature of modern culture that has been linked with depression is our quest for the new and exciting, which, for many, is a frantic flight from boredom. "Amuse me" is the theme. If we are not amused, we have the dreadful quiet to fill. As Pascal astutely noted, "I have often said that the sole cause of man's unhappiness is that he does not know how to stay quietly in his room."[6]

Boredom is a malaise that hangs over the younger generations. Perhaps it is because they have compressed sex, drugs, and money into a shorter period of time and found them unsatisfying. With nothing new to entertain them, they are dreading the decades to come. With no particular purpose, their goal is to tolerate and survive a boring, goal-less existence that will probably be less affluent than that of their parents.

The antidote for boredom is joy. It comes when our hopes are fixed on something eternally wonderful and beautiful. Augustine rightly identified the ultimate object of joy as God.

> True happiness is to rejoice in the truth, for to rejoice in the truth is to rejoice in you, O God, who are the truth . . . Those who think that there is another kind of happiness look for joy elsewhere, but theirs is not true joy.[7]

According to Augustine, true joy is the delight in the supreme beauty, goodness, and truth that are the attributes of God, of which traces may be found in the good and beautiful things of this world.

---

[6] Blaise Pascal, *Pensees* 136, tr. by A.J. Krailsheimer (London: Penguin, 1966).

[7] Augustine, *Confessions* (New York: Penguin, 1984), p. 22.

C. S. Lewis gave considerable thought to the experience of joy. He found it in small, good things such as apples, fresh air, seasons, and music. He spoke of "reading" the hand of God in our little pleasures. Like Augustine, Lewis also wanted to make it clear that joy could not rest in those things, however good.

> The books or the music in which we thought the beauty was located will betray us if we trust in them; it was not in them, it only came through them, and what came through was a longing . . . For they are not the thing itself; they are only the scent of a flower we have not found, the echo of a tune we have not heard, news from a country we have never yet visited.[8]

This longing is joy. It is a longing for glory, heaven, and, especially, God himself.

Augustine and Lewis echo Paul's exhortation to the church at Philippi to meditate on those things that are true, noble, pure, and lovely (Phil. 4:8). This exhortation resides in a letter uniquely committed to teaching the church how to have joy in the midst of suffering.

Joy is the natural response when we behold God. What does it have to do with boredom? Joyful people are mobilized. They delight in doing small obediences. They are pleased to serve God in any ordinary way he sees fit. They also know that an army of people taking small steps of obedience is what moves the kingdom of God forward in power.

---

[8] C. S. Lewis, "The Weight of Glory" in *The Weight of Glory and Other Addresses* (New York: Macmillan, 1980), p. 7.

Response

When we first listen to depression, we find that the misery is consuming. It doesn't point anywhere or say anything. It just is. But when we keep listening, it tells stories of loss, rejection, or other events that happened to the person. It speaks of identifiable physiological problems. It points to a culture of irony: the culture with the most peace, money and leisure is also the one with the most malignant sadness.

As you consider the comments about joy, don't be discouraged if joy is elusive. It takes time and practice. If, however, you don't want joy, if you are resistant to considering joy in God, then you are probably angry and avoiding God. The following chapters will give you opportunity to consider this more closely.

What feature of our culture have you absorbed that shapes your depression?

CHAPTER 13

The Heart of Depression

We are trying to carefully dissect depression. We are listening to it, hoping for clues about how it began and how it can be relieved. This led us first to highlight a number of causes that come *at* us. Satan, other people, death, and culture often play a part. The next step is to complete the loop and consider those things that come *out* of us. How do they contribute to depression (Figure 13.1)?

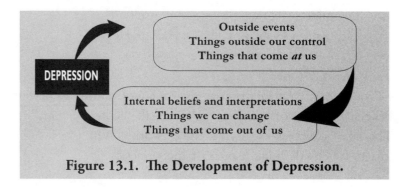

Figure 13.1. The Development of Depression.

Chapter Thirteen

Things don't simply happen to us. When they do, we respond with an immediate interpretation of their meaning and significance. We filter the event through our view of God, others and ourselves that we have been developing throughout our lives.

For example, let's say that someone didn't say hello to you at church. You interpret it: "She is angry at me;" "She is a snob;" or "She must have a lot on her mind. I need to give her a call."

It rains the entire weekend you had set aside to paint some outside woodwork. You interpret it: "I can't believe this is happening to me," which means, "I can't believe God is doing this to me." Or you might say, "I still believe that God is good even though I am disappointed. I believe he is even in these details."

These interpretations make a difference even when depression might have physical causes. Mental pain usually needs an interpretive push to send it to the hell and hopelessness we call depression. All pain is interpreted pain. With this in mind, turn your attention to what is going on within you. You will find that you are much busier than you think.

> The mind is its own place, and in itself
> Can make a Heav'n of Hell, a Hell of Heaven.[1]

Your Heart Defined

Your story, your interpretations, your motivations, and your beliefs come out of your heart. This is the center of your life. The heart oversees the "whys." Why work? Why play? Why love? It is *the* defining feature of humanness.

---

[1] John Milton, *Paradise Lost* (New York, NY: Penguin, 1968), 1:249-55, p. 54.

Above all else, guard your heart, for it is the wellspring of life. (Prov. 4:23)

Out of the overflow of the heart the mouth speaks. (Matt. 12:34)

The good man brings good things out of the good stored up in his heart, and the evil man brings evil things out of the evil stored up in his heart. (Luke 6:45)

As you can guess by this point, when you get to the farthest reaches of the human heart, you will find that it has everything to do with God. All life is lived *coram deo* (before the face of God). This doesn't mean that we are always *conscious* of God. Teens who violate parental commands rarely perceive their infractions as personal attacks against their parents. They are thinking, *I want to go my own way. I want independence. My disobedience is 'nothing personal.'*

All of life, however, is personal. At some level, all people know God (Rom. 1:21). We don't just have a fuzzy idea that there is a god, gods or "higher power" out there somewhere. Within the human heart, there is a personal knowledge of the God who is, and we are either trusting him or something else. To use more religious language, we are either worshiping him, or we are worshiping idols such as pleasure, money, success, and love. Ultimately, the heart is either/or.

Who do you love? God or the world? (Deut. 6:5; 1 John 2:15)
Who do you trust? God or people? (Jer. 17:5-8)
Who (or what) do you worship? God or gods? (2 Kings 17:36)

Who will you serve? God or money? (Matt. 6:24)

Who do you obey? God or the Devil? (1 John 3:10)

For whose glory do you live? God's or your own? (Rom. 1:21-23)

Where is your treasure? In God or the world? (Matt. 6:21)

To whom do you belong? To God or Satan? (John 8:44)

Some teenagers who have been raised in church have very self-consciously turned away from God. They know God exists, and they even believe the gospel is true, but they want to go their own way. Their allegiances are to their own desires rather than God.

Some people might not think about God at all. They don't consciously deny him or acknowledge him. Their hearts, however, are revealed when they are suddenly angry with God for bringing some difficulty into their lives. For example, a hard-working businessman considered himself a-religious – he just didn't think about God. But on the day his business burned to the ground, he cursed God and vowed never to enter a church for the rest of his life. He knew that God existed.

Some people claim to be atheists. They have thought about whether or not God exists and chosen to believe that there is no God. But here again the heart will be revealed. You might find a profound fear of death, consultations with palm-readers, or a mid-life crisis that indicates purposelessness. (Any question about purpose is a religious question.)

Whoever we are and whatever we believe, we are all structured the same. We see our actions; more hidden are our thoughts and feelings. Beneath those are our imaginations and motivations – the apparent reasons for our thoughts, feelings, and actions. But deeper still is the knowledge of God and our response to him (Figure 13.2).

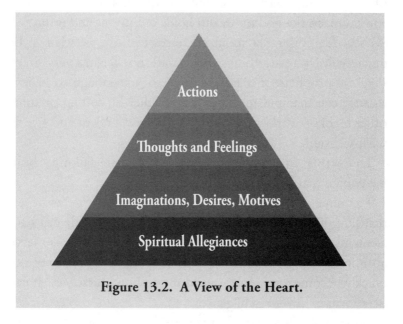

Figure 13.2. A View of the Heart.

The Natural Inclination of the Heart

Our hearts, as we have seen, are out of kilter. This is no surprise to you because your entire life feels out of kilter. But there is a specific way our hearts are misaligned. They were intended to be devoted to God, but they aren't. Instead, they are devoted to a strange brew of God, ourselves and the objects of our affections, a.k.a., our idols.

Why this misplaced and compromised devotion?

We are proud. It might not make any sense at first, especially when you feel so low, but our hearts are proud. Since ancient times, people have bowed down to idols in the appearance of humility and contrition. But their goal wasn't to be mastered by the idol. People worship to *get* things. We choose idols in part because we believe that they will give us what we want. The god

127

of drugs brings fearlessness, the god of sex promises pleasure and intimacy, the god of wealth holds out power and influence. We can feel miserable about ourselves because we want to be great, at least at *some*thing, and we are not feeling very great. Like the prophets of Baal, we are arrogant enough to believe that we can manipulate the idol – whether by cutting or some other form of works righteousness – so it will relent and give us what we want.

Does this fit your experience? We are talking about something that is universal.

Examine your imaginations and fantasies. Don't they reveal that hint of self-exaltation? Even thoughts of suicide can have elements of pride. Suicide will stop pain, but it will also leave an imprint on the minds of others. Even lowly self-pity can quickly become a reason for us to think about ourselves. It can be a form of proud indulgence.

You may be depressed, but you are still a person, and people, by nature, have proud streaks throughout.

We crave autonomy. Autonomy is closely linked to arrogance. They are both expressions of human pride, but autonomy suggests that we want to be *separate from* more than *over*. We want to establish the rules rather than submit to the lordship of the living God. This was the essence of Adam's original sin. We want to interpret the world according to *our* system of thought. We want to establish our own parallel universe, separate from God's.

One popular expression of autonomy is American deism. Deism is not a formal church or denomination, but it is arguably the most popular belief system in the United States. Deism acknowledges God, but it believes that he is far off, too preoccupied to be involved in daily affairs. Its mottoes are "God helps those who help themselves" and similar principles that avoid trust or faith as the primary human response to God.

In Deism we can settle the frontier without anyone meddling in our business.

Can you see this in depression? Part of the depressive syndrome is that you are immensely loyal to your interpretation of yourself and your world. If God says you are forgiven in Christ, you create new rules that mandate contrition, penance, and self-loathing. If God says he loves you, you insist it is impossible. There it is: your system is higher than God's.

The way out of autonomy begins with a simple prayer. "Lord, teach me. I want to think like you." Just think what it would be like to be certain that the God of the universe loved you. That alone would probably change the contours of depression.

We want to indulge our desires. But pride and autonomy are not all that's wrong with our hearts. Both point to the fact that we are grasping, desiring creatures. We want something. We covet. We want *more* (Eph. 4:19). And we are jealous of those who have what we want.

"I want! I want more!" More security, more love, more peace, more money, more respect, more freedom, more money, more beauty, and so on. Think about it for a moment. Does it seem that more of anything would change your depression? If so, you are most likely seeing the grasping, accumulating desires of the human heart.

The problem is that even if we *get* more, we never feel quite satisfied, so we want more still. Even God is not enough. Then, when more is not available, life becomes empty and holds no interest.

Needs and Allegiances

Many depressed people have been hurt and rejected by others. They feel as though basic relational needs have not been met, and they will be stuck in depression until they are. Rejection from parents, spouses, or friends has left a profound emptiness that feels like an emotional handicap. What does this have to do with the heart?

Consider first the example of Jesus. He is God, but he was truly human. If anything is clear from his life, he didn't get love from people, he never prayed that he would know the love of other people, and he didn't seem emotionally undone by rejection and misunderstanding. Rather, his deepest needs, as noted in his prayers, were for the glory of his Father to be revealed and for his spiritual children to be protected from the evil one and united in love (John 17).

The desire to be loved is natural. If you don't have that desire, something is wrong. Yet there is something deeper still. This unmet desire does not quite go to the core of our being. We can go a step further and ask, *Why do I feel this need for love? What is it really saying?*

The desire for love is good. The problem is that, left unchecked, it never stops growing. Keep in mind that our hearts keep repeating the chorus, "I want." We want more love, and more again. It is here that you observe the spiritual roots.

There are times when we put our trust in a person (something created) and what we can get from that person *rather than* putting our trust in Christ and loving others. Once again, it comes down to spiritual allegiances. Like the ancient idolaters, we have said that God is not enough.

The feeling of emptiness is usually a sign that we have put our trust in something that can't sustain us. It reminds us that we were created to trust in our heavenly Father and nothing else. We were created to enjoy the many things God gives without making them the center of our lives. When we confuse the two, our lives feel out of kilter. To feel better, we try again and search for love apart from God, but when we finally realize that it is elusive, we forsake the quest and quietly despair.

Keep probing. Life is ultimately about God.

When you get to God, don't stop until he surprises you with his beauty and love, which shouldn't take too long. After all, if you can find mixed allegiances, dual allegiances, spiritual unfaithfulness, or a wandering heart in your life, you are essentially guilty of spiritual adultery, and, contrary to your expectations, your God delights in your return (Luke 15:11-24).

Response

As you consider your own heart more carefully, please keep two things in mind. First, don't think that this means that your sin is causing your depression. It is true that you will find sin – that is an essential part of our walk with Jesus. In times of suffering, Scripture encourages us to "throw off everything that hinders and the sin that so easily entangles" (Heb. 12:1). You should be concerned if you *don't* see sin, because one of the ways the Holy Spirit loves us is by revealing sin. Since sin is what really corrupts life and everything good, we are blessed when we can see it and turn from it. But this doesn't automatically mean that sin is the cause of your depression.

Second, keep Christ close on this part of the path. Keep Psalm 130 close. The heart of Scripture is that God has moved toward us and taken the initiative to forgive our sins. He doesn't forgive because you are sad about your sin; he forgives because Jesus paid the penalty in full.

The curious path to true life is to grow in both the knowledge of God's love and your own sin.

While I regarded God as a tyrant, I thought my sin a trifle, but when I knew him to be my Father, then I mourned that I could ever have kicked against him.[2]

Pascal offered this wise summary:

Knowing God without knowing our own wretchedness makes for pride.
Knowing our own wretchedness without knowing God makes for despair.
Knowing Jesus Christ strikes the balance because he shows us both God and our own wretchedness.[3]

What do you see in your own heart?

---

[2] Charles H. Spurgeon, "Repentance After Conversion," *The Metropolitan Tabernacle Pulpit*, vol. 41 (London: Banner of Truth, 1895), sermon #2419.

[3] Blaise Pascal, *Pensees*, trans A.J. Krailsheimer (London: Penguin, 1966), no. 192.

CHAPTER 14

The Heart Unveiled

One of the problems with the heart is that it is hard to know it. We can quickly list the circumstances of life that shape who we are, such as family, friends, and teachers, but the heart tends to hide, both from ourselves and others. Knowing about it and knowing it are two different things.

Here are a series of questions we can ask to discover what is in our heart.

What do you love? What do you hate?
What do you want, crave, hope for?
What is your goal?
What do you fear?
What do you worry about?
What do you feel like you need?
Where do you find refuge, comfort, pleasure or security?
Who are your heroes and role models?
What defines success or failure for you?
When do you say, "If only ...."? (e.g., "If only my

husband would ...")
What do you see as your rights?
What do you pray for?
What do you talk about?
What are your dreams or fantasies?
When do you get angry?
When do you tend to doubt Scripture?
Where in your life have you struggled with bitterness?
What or whom do you avoid?
Do you feel guilty at times?[1]

Under ordinary circumstances we rarely ask these questions of ourselves or allow them to take us to the spiritual core of our lives, but depression is not an ordinary circumstance. Depression unveils our hearts.

Isn't it true that suffering reveals us? While prosperity allows us to hide, hardships peel off masks we didn't even know we were wearing. During the better times, we can be happy, unafraid, confident and optimistic, but the lean years reveal the best and the worst in us. Put a dozen relatively like-minded people into the same crisis and you will see a dozen different responses. Some are heroes, others are cowards. Some are leaders, others are followers. Some are optimistic, others despair. Some shake their fist at God, others quietly submit. You don't really know who you are until you have gone through suffering. We can measure our spiritual growth by the way we behave under pressure.

Throughout history, God has used hardships to reveal people's hearts, and this unveiling has had a purpose. It is an

---

[1] David Powlison, *Basic Biblical Concepts of Human Motivation*, unpublished. Also see, Paul Tripp, "Opening blind eyes: Another look at data gathering," *Journal of Biblical Counseling*, 14:2, 1996, pp. 6-11.

essential part of the process of change. You have to see what is in your heart before you can set out to change it.

Notice how those who have medicated away their hardships with illegal drugs, alcohol or sex can seem immature. They may look forty-five but they have the character of an adolescent. Find a person who has weathered storms rather than avoided them and you will find someone who is wise.

Personal growth and change are not always easy, but they are essential to true humanness. It is simply how we were built. They are the Creator's intent. You can see it taking place in animals, plants, and people. Everything alive grows. The difference with human beings is that we grow physically *and* spiritually.

When we grow in the right direction, it is right and good. The Hebrew word *shalom* captures it: peace, wholeness, realignment rather than dislocation. Spiritual growth just feels right. In fact, it is a blessing that can make depression feel less oppressive. Depression can feel like the severe pain of someone dying of cancer, but it can also be like the pain of surgery, which indicates that we are getting better. If both pains could be physically measured, they might be identical in their intensity, at least to a researcher. But the pain from surgery will seem less severe to the sufferer than the pain of cancer. The pain from surgery is making you better; the other is a sign that you are worse.

When we see something of our own hearts, we are in a position to grow and change. However hard it is to have our innermost being exposed, it is a necessary part of the path of blessing.

This unveiling might yield other benefits as well. It might reveal things in our hearts that have contributed to the depression itself. There is no way to be certain that our hearts are the primary cause of our depression, but when we work on the issues that depression reveals, the pain can sometimes lift because we have found one of its causes. In other words, the problem behind depression is not always physical. Many depression experts have come to a similar conclusion.

For example, one popular approach to depression is called cognitive therapy. It focuses on the way people think. Is everything white or black, all or nothing, an opportunity or an obstacle? These ways of thinking lie relatively dormant during calmer times, but they are unmistakably active during depression. The goal of cognitive therapy is to identify these "thinking errors," change them, and, in so doing, hopefully alleviate the depression. This school of thought suggests that these thinking errors are not just *revealed* by depression, they actually *cause* it. Therefore, when you change your thinking, you change your depression. Brain scans even show that we can bring about significant physical changes in our brains simply by thinking differently.

My point is that we are taking a path that is not far-fetched or implausible. It bears similarities to the better known theories about depression. It is not unusual to think that depression can reveal us and that we bring something to depression. What is unique about what we are saying is that we are going even deeper: we are going beyond thinking errors to consider errors in the way we know God.

Detours in the Wilderness

The principle that suffering tests us and reveals our hearts is one that appears throughout Scripture. You first see it when the Israelites leave Egypt, a key episode in biblical history. Here God demonstrated that he was not simply a local tribal god. He was the Creator God who rules over all things, including Egypt and its Pharaoh. To emphasize this point, God used Moses, an unqualified orator, as his representative, and delivered Israel from Egyptian bondage without a warrior unsheathing a sword.

Before the people were given access to the land God promised them, Moses led them across a desert wilderness. It was not an easy trek, but God's purpose was to reveal his patience, kindness, and care. He also intended to test them, to see — or have them see — what was in their hearts.

> Remember how the LORD your God led you all the way in the desert these forty years, to humble you and to test you in order to know what was in your heart, whether or not you would keep his commands. (Deut. 8:2)

The people failed the test repeatedly. When water supplies were low, they grumbled against the Lord rather than trusted him. When they were eager for meat and bread, they grumbled against the Lord rather than trusted him. In trial after trial, they failed to trust. But it wasn't until they refused to enter the Promised Land because they feared its inhabitants more than they trusted God that God extended their stay in the wilderness for forty years.

From then on, the wilderness or desert theme recurs in Scripture as part of the journey through which God guides nearly all his people. During this journey, people's hearts are revealed. Abraham, Joseph, Daniel, and many others went through the desert and were revealed as people of faith. They trusted in the Lord during their wilderness journeys. Aaron, King Ahaz, and Jonah trusted in themselves.

The desert biographies of Scripture climax when "Jesus was led by the Spirit into the desert to be tempted by the devil" (Matt. 4:1). He replicated the Israelites' desert journey (one day for each of their years) and exceeded their hunger by his forty day fast. Jesus then was taken through the most rigorous trials and testing by Satan himself. The outcome, however, was never in doubt. Jesus' heart never wavered. Regardless of the physical pain or the temptations before him, Jesus trusted in his Father to deliver him. In doing so, he becomes our model, our hope, and our power when we are in the desert. When we fail in our desert trials, we can point to Jesus' success in his. His victories are ours through faith, so his story becomes our own when we trust him.

Joy in the Desert?

It is in the context of desert trials that the book of James says this:

> Consider it pure joy, my brothers, whenever you face trials of many kinds, because you know that the testing of your faith develops perseverance. Perseverance must finish its work so that you may be mature and complete, not lacking anything. (James 1:2-4)

Joy and suffering are wedded together. At first glance it looks like an impossible marriage, but James is not the only one to speak about hardships with a hint of a smile on his face. Other Scriptures concur.

> Now for a little while you may have had to suffer grief in all kinds of trials. These have come so that your faith – of greater worth than gold . . . – may be proved genuine and may result in praise, glory and honor when Jesus Christ is revealed. (1 Peter 1:6-7)

Before Jesus came, wise people willingly endured difficulties because they knew God was with them. After the cross everything was transformed, including perspectives on suffering. Pilgrim travelers still encounter suffering as much as ever, but suffering is now viewed as the pains of childbirth rather than pain that is purposeless and random – mere accidents. Since Jesus came, suffering is redemptive. When we keep Jesus in view, the one who "learned obedience from what he suffered" (Heb. 5:8), we can begin to understand how James could encourage us to have joy in the desert trek.

If you think that Scripture is not up to speed on real life – that saints spend their time thinking about the next life rather than dealing with the present – then read the book of James. James is highly practical; he is familiar with suffering and persecution. He is savvy about real life. His counsel is given not to mystics who shun the world but to ordinary people who have to face it.

Notice why he is excited about trials: trials, he writes, have a purpose. They test our faith. They reveal what we worship, what we trust, what we love. From James's perspective, this is evidence of God's fatherly care. It is essential to our spiritual welfare. It would be a tragedy to go through life with a nominal faith we *think* is genuine but isn't. God's love is behind the trials that reveal the true condition of our faith. His desire is that we become "mature and complete, not lacking anything." In other words, when our faith is refined so that we learn to trust God in all things, we will be satisfied in him above all else. We won't need the traditional accoutrements of life. Christ will be enough. For James, this growth process is so glorious that it can provoke us to joy.

Listen to other wise teachers who have suffered:

In heaviness we often learn lessons that we never could attain elsewhere. Do you know that God has beauties for every part of the world, and He has beauties for every place of experience? There are views to be seen from the tops of the Alps...but there are beauties to be seen in the depths of the dell that you could never see from the tops of mountains . . . Ah, said Luther, affliction is the best book in my library, the best leaf is the leaf of heaviness.[2]

This has dramatic implications for the struggle with depression. James does not naïvely assume that our hardships will be over this side of heaven. He assumes that they will continue. People will be depressed and they might become depressed again. But James presents an emotional experience that is difficult to describe: joy, he writes, can be present during any wilderness experience. Joy wasn't as accessible during the Israelites' original journey because everything was new and uncertain. They didn't understand the ways of God, and they weren't confident in his goodness and power. But the cross can wipe out any doubt. Now, on this end of history, we can actually sing songs with joy when we are in the wilderness.

Joy is not the opposite of depression. It is deeper than depression. Therefore, you can experience both. Depression is the relentless rain. Joy is the rock. Whether depression is present or not, you can stand on joy.

Does all this seem unattainable? Are you more hopeless when you read it? If so, treat these verses like the Psalms: even if they don't capture your present experience, let them be a vision for what lies ahead. This is what God wants to give you. Pray that

---

[2] E. R. Skoglund, *Bright Days, Dark Nights* (Grand Rapids: Baker, 2000), pp. 86-87.

this passage would more and more be your own. Pray that God would receive glory by giving you joy in the midst of your trials.

Response

Your simple prayer can be, "Search me."

> Search me, O God, and know my heart;
> test me and know my anxious thoughts.
> See if there is any offensive way in me,
> and lead me in the way everlasting.
> (Ps. 139:23-24)

Life before God is an ongoing sequence of living, evaluating, and changing, then re-evaluating and changing, then re-evaluating and changing. Depression too is an occasion for re-evaluating and changing.

Fear

Listen to descriptions of depression and you will often hear words like "desperation," "panic," "abandonment," "anxieties," and "dread." You will hear allusions to hell, and hell is always associated with profound fear. When depression is at its most severe, paranoia is one of its cardinal features. It is fear run amok. It can feel as if both you and your world are falling apart, and you are certain there is nothing you can do about it.

What do fearful people do when they feel powerless? They avoid. They withdraw. Their world becomes smaller and smaller. In other words, they act depressed.

When fears are left unattended, they can lead to depression. You can try to avoid them when they haunt you, but you can still feel them. The only way to really quiet them is to confront them. And since fears run in packs, expect to find more than one.

You may find that you are terrified to:

- make a wrong decision
- fail

- die
- suffer
- be exposed
- lose a loved one
- lose money, a job, or other forms of security
- be abandoned, rejected or alone
- not have control

Apart from depression, fears may lie dormant; with it, they are revealed. Sometimes, however, depressed people don't recognize their fear. Fearful people seem agitated and restless, while depression is more typically expressed in passivity and resignation. So listen carefully to your heart. Find your fears. They might be contributing to the feelings of depression, and there is much that can be done to alleviate them.

Common Fears

When you start to list your biggest fears, you will quickly recognize that you are not alone with them. We are people given to fear. Here are a few of the more common ones.

Fear of death. Fear of death affects us much more than we know. Imagine how different your life would be if you experienced absolutely no fear of death. Even if you are confident that you will be with Jesus, the unknown is always intimidating and Scripture doesn't give many specifics. Even when we are looking forward to something, we might be a little nervous about the unpredictable details. This is intensified with depression. Many depressed people lack confidence that they will be with Jesus, so their fears can be even more intense.

Will all your sins be exposed? Will God be displeased? Did you believe "enough"?

Anticipating these concerns, God speaks clearly and

frequently about how to be certain of eternal matters. The letter of 1 John is devoted to it, and all the New Testament writers discuss it.

Fear of the way you will die. Most people can acknowledge a fear of how death will come. Will it be long and painful? Will it be quick and painless? Will you be alone? If you have witnessed a difficult death, these fears are likely to be more pronounced. And, like other fears, when these are left unattended, they can develop into depression. Now is the time to hear God's words and believe him when he says that he will give you the grace when you need it.

Fear of the past recurring. If you have had an especially difficult past, it might control you more than you think. Your emotions don't discriminate very well between past and present. Even though it might be impossible to re-experience the same past hurts, your feelings tell you otherwise. The danger can seem present tense. You are always on guard. Here is where many of the psalms are especially valuable, because they are written by and for people who are facing a threat.

Fear from trusting in things that don't last. Perhaps the most common fear arises when the things we trust in become unsteady and begin to topple.

If you trust in your physical beauty, it will accommodate your trust for a time. But what happens when plastic surgery can't rid you of all the wrinkles, and your body sags no matter what you do to it?

If you trust in financial security, what will happen if you lose your job? Don't you always feel like you need more than you have?

If you trust in a person, what if he dies? What if she is less than perfect in giving you affection? What if he leaves?

Or perhaps your trust isn't in one person in particular. The problem is that you trust in *people*. Your goal has been to please, and you are finding such a goal increasingly impossible to achieve.

If your trust is invested in anything other than Jesus, fear will eventually reign. And when fear's reign continues, it invites depression to rule with it.

THE Question Again

Regardless of the particular fear you have, fear always asks the same questions: "Who will you trust? Where will you turn when you are afraid or anxious?" The story of Scripture is one in which God demonstrates himself to be trustworthy, and then he invites wary people to trust him. Given such an attractive invitation, you would think that none could resist, but we all have our reasons for putting our trust in things we can see.

The Shepherd Is Present

In spite of our reluctance, God delights in speaking words of hope and comfort to fearful people. He reserves some of the most beautiful revelations of himself for the timid. He patiently reasons with them. He reminds them that he is God, and he promises that he will never leave them alone. He shares with them some of his names – the ones that only intimate friends know.

> O my *Strength*, I watch for you; you, O God, are my fortress, my loving God. (Ps. 59:9-10)

> My *shield* is God Most High. (Ps. 7:10)

> The LORD is my *rock*, my *fortress* . . . *the horn of my salvation*, my *stronghold*. (Ps. 18:2)

The best known name is Shepherd. The best known psalm for those who are afraid is Psalm 23. Its New Testament counterpart, which is actually spoken by the Good Shepherd, is Jesus' teaching on worry in the Sermon on the Mount (Matt. 5-7).

You are probably familiar with this passage, but read it carefully. These are God's words to you. Notice how Jesus never tires of repeating his promises. Instead, he patiently reasons with fearful people. He is persuading you to trust him.

> Then Jesus said to his disciples: "Therefore I tell you, do not worry about your life, what you will eat; or about your body, what you will wear. Life is more than food, and the body more than clothes. Consider the ravens: They do not sow or reap, they have no storeroom or barn; yet God feeds them. And how much more valuable you are than birds! Who of you by worrying can add a single hour to his life? Since you cannot do this very little thing, why do you worry about the rest?
>
> "Consider how the lilies grow. They do not labor or spin. Yet I tell you, not even Solomon in all his splendor was dressed like one of these. If that is how God clothes the grass of the field, which is here today, and tomorrow is thrown into the fire, how much more will he clothe you, O you of little faith! And do not set your heart on what you will eat or drink; do not worry about it. For the pagan world runs after all such things, and your Father knows that you need them. But seek his kingdom, and these things will be given to you as well.
>
> "Do not be afraid, little flock, for your Father has been pleased to give you the kingdom. Sell your

possessions and give to the poor. Provide purses for yourselves that will not wear out, a treasure in heaven that will not be exhausted, where no thief comes near and no moth destroys. For where your treasure is, there your heart will be also." (Luke 12:22-34)

How incredibly tender! How patient. He calls us his little flock, aware that life holds many dangers. He reminds us that the Creator knows the details of his creation. He is close and involved. He knows the needs of common ravens; he knows when a petal falls from the lily. If he knows these details about things that are not created in his image, how much more will he care for you? In God's eyes, you are much more valuable than the rest of creation.

And he is not just interested in the big picture of your life. He knows trivia such as the hairs on your head (Luke 12:7). To have that kind of knowledge, someone must be present with the person and have immense care for him or her. Casual acquaintances are satisfied with knowing the basic outline of your life. Intimate friends want to know all the details.

Then Jesus asks, with tongue in cheek, if anxiety really helps. Can it make you grow? Can it give you more money? Jesus is suggesting that the situation is not as dire as we think. He can make light of it because he knows that there is no need to worry. He is the loving shepherd. He will not leave, and he will never sleep (Ps. 121:4).

"You trust me," he says. "I will worry about tomorrow." Then, in a beautiful and persuasive conclusion, he reminds us that he is a generous God who not only gives the kingdom to his children but is *pleased* to do so.

This raises two questions. First, what is the kingdom? The kingdom is everything God promises his children: love, joy, peace, his presence, forgiveness, adoption into his family, the hope of being free from sin, and being with our Father, the King.

Second, is the kingdom important to you? Perhaps you already believe that God is pleased to give you the kingdom, but the kingdom doesn't sound that great. Perhaps you have your heart set on something else. You believe that "my God will meet all your needs according to his glorious riches in Christ Jesus" (Phil. 4:19), but you aren't so certain that he will supply all your *wants*.

This is how idolatry grows in our hearts. We want things and we aren't sure God will give them to us, so we put our trust in other gods. This is THE problem of the human heart – misplaced trust. We value, love and trust something in creation more than the Creator, and since there is nothing in creation that is intended to bear the weight of our trust, we are bound to live in fear.

All other loves must be subordinate to your love for Christ. This may sound like God is demanding our love, and that is true to a point. But the *reason* we are to love him more than all others is that, among the many suitors for our affections, he alone is worthy of such love.

How do you turn back to the One who truly loves you? It is called repentance. You acknowledge your wrong in pursuing false gods, and you set out to know the beauty of the true God who patiently pursues you.

Learning from Manna

Another feature common to most fears is that they are more concerned about the future than the present. "I think tragedy is *coming*." We predict the future, and we cling tenaciously to our prophecies.

149

Some people specialize in these anxieties, others merely dabble in them, but we all indulge in them. This is why one of the first lessons God taught his people was about anxiety and trust.

When the Israelites were in the desert, food was scarce, so it was the ideal place to learn how to trust. To feed the hundreds of thousands of Israelites, God rained down a kind of bread each day (Ex. 16), but he only gave enough for one day (except for the day before the Sabbath, when they were given enough for two). This established a spiritual rhythm. They did what God told them to do *today*, and they trusted him for tomorrow. Those who trusted in themselves and collected for more than one day found that their surplus manna turned to maggots by morning. They quickly learned that faith in the true God was the only way to live.

Undoubtedly, the first couple days were the hardest. The people woke up hungry, saw that there was no food in the tent, and hadn't yet looked outside. Would the manna be there this morning? Would God be faithful to his promises? Over time, however, they became confident. They learned that God would care for them tomorrow because he had said he would, and he had been faithful the day before.

This is the backdrop for Jesus' words of comfort, "but seek his kingdom [today], and these things will be given to you as well [tomorrow]." Your goal is to get into a manna rhythm. Seek his grace today, be faithful to the tasks in front of you, and trust him for tomorrow. Then, when you look back and see that he was faithful, your faith will be "fed" for the next day.

"I Will Be with You"

Still afraid? Jesus anticipates that we are going to struggle with fear rather than have it instantly disappear. In response, he reminds us that he will never leave us.

"Do not be afraid, for I am with you." (Gen. 26:24)

"Do not be afraid or terrified because of them, for the LORD your God goes with you; he will never leave you nor forsake you." (Deut. 31:6)

"Do not fear, for I am with you; do not be dismayed, for I am your God." (Isa. 41:10)

But Zion said, "The LORD has forsaken me, the Lord has forgotten me." "Can a mother forget the baby at her breast and have no compassion on the child she has borne? Though she may forget, I will not forget you! See, I have engraved you on the palms of my hands; your walls are ever before me." (Isa. 49:14-16)

"I will ask the Father, and he will give you another Counselor, to be with you forever – the Spirit of truth. . . he lives with you and will be in you. I will not leave you as orphans." (John 14:16-18)

Imagine the presence of one who deeply loves you and is powerful enough to deal with the things you fear. It turns fear into confidence. But, like all spiritual growth, this change only comes with practice. It comes when you say, "Amen – I believe" when you hear or read the promises of God. It comes through meditation on God's words. It comes when the cross of Jesus Christ assures you that God is faithful.

These words to the fearful are so important that Jesus makes them his final words on earth: "And surely I am with you always, to the very end of the age" (Matt. 28:20). The resurrection is God's answer to fear. Jesus is alive.

Response

Fears are loud and demanding. Even when you know they are irrational, they can still control you. It is hard to argue with feelings that are so intense, and easy to be loyal to our inaccurate interpretations. So don't expect to be writing any psalms of victory just yet. Instead, claim as your own some of the psalms that are journals of fear. For example, Psalm 46 talks about treacherous circumstances, but it still keeps circling around to the same refrain: "The LORD Almighty is with us; the God of Jacob is our fortress" (Ps. 46:7, 11). Psalm 56 describes being slandered and attacked, but the psalmist calms his heart: "When I am afraid, I will trust in you" (Ps. 56:3). As you meditate on some of the psalms that speak about fear, you will find that you, too, will be able to make quicker transitions from fear to faith (see Psalm 57:4-5).

There are two basic steps in dealing with fears. First, confess them as unbelief. Isn't it true that much of our fear is our hearts saying, "Lord, I don't believe you," or "Lord, my desires want something other than what you promised"? Second, examine Scripture and be confident in the love and faithfulness of Jesus. Ask someone who is confident in Jesus to give reasons for his or her confidence.

What are your fears? Where is your trust?

CHAPTER 16

Anger

Fear is the most obvious co-conspirator with depression; anger is the most common. The formula is a simple one:

$$Sadness + Anger = Depression.$$

Most people can find their anger easily, but sometimes you have to look in unanticipated places.

"Why can't you believe that you are forgiven?"

This thirty-five-year-old woman had been depressed for ten years and made two suicide attempts. Like many depressed people, everything about her said self-loathing. On this occasion she was describing the guilt she felt for having said something hurtful to her sister. You could actually see her weighed down by it.

Her answer was shocking.

"If I believe that God forgives me, then I will have to forgive my father, and I could never do that." Her anger was obvious, surprising even herself.

Yes, she was guilty, but her guilt went deeper than she thought. She was guilty for standing in judgment over her father, whose sins in this case were minimal. She did not believe that God was going to be harsh enough on him, so she appointed herself as the judge, jury and executioner. The fact that this meant that she would have to deny grace and mercy for herself was a small price to pay for the satisfaction of judging him.

Anger will not always be the cause of your depression, although some researchers want to tell you that it is a *likely* cause. But anger is frequently revealed by depression. The wisest way to approach this subject is to assume that you are angry. Anger is as basic to our condition as bipedal locomotion and opposable thumbs. If you are a person with a mind and emotions, you will find anger.

To make this search even more important, remember that anger *hides*. The angry person is always the last person to know that he or she is angry. We will acknowledge that we are depressed, fearful, or in pain, but we are blind to our anger. Anger is always another person's problem, not our own.

Finding Anger

Anger includes a broad spectrum of behaviors. It can contribute to depression even when you don't remember a particular cause. Like the Hatfields and the McCoys, neither party remembers what originally started the feud, but they know they are supposed to be angry at one another.

A few questions can help uncover the root.

> What are my personal needs? "Needs" are usually a euphemism for "rights" and "demands."
> Where have my needs been unmet?

Where have my rights been violated?
What do I think I deserve that I haven't received?
Of whom am I jealous?

If you limit your awareness of anger to overt rage, you will miss it. Violent anger is just one expression of anger (Figure 16.1).

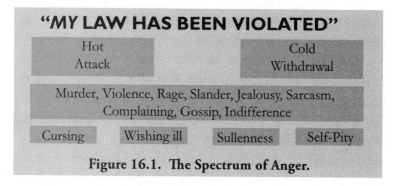

"MY LAW HAS BEEN VIOLATED"

Hot	Cold
Attack	Withdrawal

Murder, Violence, Rage, Slander, Jealousy, Sarcasm, Complaining, Gossip, Indifference

| Cursing | Wishing ill | Sullenness | Self-Pity |

Figure 16.1. The Spectrum of Anger.

A depressed man said nothing to his wife for one year – not one word. In public he related normally. He elicited sympathy because he didn't have a job. His rationale for his "quietness" was that he was depressed. But sadness can cover rage.

Anger can be either hot or cold. People are as hurt by one as they are by the other. The main difference is that hot anger is brief and explosive, cold settles in long-term. Depressive anger is usually cold: the "cold shoulder," withdrawal, calculated rejection, putting blame on others, feeling sorry for oneself. In some ways, it is the most extreme anger in that it refuses to be affected by the other person. "I have been hurt, and I will never care enough to be hurt again." Avoid the hot-tempered person, but tremble before the cold, distant, uncaring, angry person.

Chapter Sixteen

The Heart of Anger

Anger says, "You have done wrong." It is making some kind of judgment, and the judgment is often accurate. Anger might be responding to a real wrong. But this is only the beginning of the story. Once anger settles in, it will bring you to an increasingly familiar crossroad.

Will you turn to the true God, who shows compassion to those who have been victimized, or will you trust yourself?

Will you turn to the true God, who is the holy and righteous judge, or will you form a vigilante party that meets in your name, for your sake, and for your glory?

Anger typically begins in a way that imitates God – it makes judgments about right and wrong. But it can quickly turn into a stance against him. You are angry because your rights and your glory – not God's – have been violated.

This is where you must be an expert in knowing your own heart. Otherwise you are left groping in the dark. What you can see about anger is that someone did wrong and you are angry. What you *don't* see is that the anger reveals more about your own heart than it does about the other person. To be more specific, anger is between you and God.

Take grumbling as an example. Who hasn't grumbled and complained in the last couple of days? Grumbling or complaining fits within the larger category of anger because it is a judgment. The grumbler has declared something to be wrong, be it a person, the weather, or the expensive car repair. Usually, it is directed at no one in particular. It is just a complaint. While those who are overtly angry might shake their fist at God, God rarely is mentioned during low-level grumbling or complaining.

But grumbling is more about us than it is about other people or our circumstances. It is our hearts saying something against God. When Israel was hungry during its journey through the desert, "the whole community grumbled against Moses and Aaron" (Ex. 16:2). That, however, is only the one-dimensional picture. It sees the horizontal but not the vertical. The people needed Moses's spiritual insights to see more. "'You are not grumbling against us,' Moses replied, 'but against the LORD'" (Ex. 16:8).

Soon after this, they complained against Moses about not having water. Moses once again diagnosed the problem immediately. Water was not the issue. The problem was their hearts. "'Why do you put the LORD to the test?'" (Ex. 17:2).

Moses was making a serious indictment. He knew that God tested the hearts of his people to see if they would follow him during more threatening conditions. That was God's prerogative, and it taught his people to trust him. But for the people to test God! Moses charged them with standing over God in judgment.

Do you see the role reversal in anger? God has a right to test our hearts. Who are we to test God and question him? It is the height of arrogance. Indeed, our circumstances can be very difficult, but God is God. He has the right to do anything he wants.

This seminal story challenges us to be on guard. During difficult times, we can still blindly follow the mob and test God without even knowing it.

"OK, God, are you present or not? Show me. Show me by _____. And if you don't show me here and now, I will not trust you."

Of course, we don't say this openly, but if we really listen to our grumbling, we will detect words against God.

Knowing God

When you dig deep, anger is about spiritual allegiances. Who will you trust? Our anger indicates that we really don't trust God. Therefore, when we identify anger in our lives, we can't simply say, "I am going to stop being angry." Such a resolution is admirable, but it is a shortcut that is doomed to fail. Anger is ultimately about God. It shows that we don't trust him, and it becomes an opportunity to know him better. What you come to understand will surprise you.

God is who you imitate. God tells us, "Be holy, because I am holy" (Lev. 11:44). If you really want to know what it means to be truly human, learn to imitate God.

God, as you know, is no namby-pamby. He hates dishonest scales (Prov. 20:10), evil (8:13), haughty eyes, a lying tongue, murderers, schemers, false witnesses, those who stir up dissension (6:16-19). He hates the injustices that can be found in divorce (Mal. 2:16). He hates hypocrisy, especially among the leaders of the people (Mark 3:5). He was indignant when the disciples rebuked the little children (Mark 10:14). There is indeed a time for hatred and anger (Eccl. 3:8).

But don't get the wrong impression. God's anger is an expression of his love. If you don't get angry, you don't love. If you witness injustice and are unmoved, you do not love the victim. So if God hates dishonesty, he loves honesty. If he hates haughty eyes, he loves humility; a lying tongue, truthfulness; murderers, those who build others up; schemers and false witnesses, peacemaking.

Why does God love these things? Everything God loves is a reflection of his own character. *He* is honest, humble, truthful and peacemaking. When we love what he loves, it is a sign that we are becoming more like him, as God intended us to be.

When we think of anger, we usually picture someone losing his temper. That can never be the picture of God's anger. God never loses his temper. Instead, when he reveals his anger, he leaves it on simmer (Ex. 32:9-10, 14). He invites his people to return and reason with him (Isa. 1:18), and he can quickly be persuaded to turn from his anger. For now, God has chosen to place his anger within limits. "'In a surge of anger I hid my face from you for a moment; but with everlasting kindness I will have compassion on you,' says the LORD, your Redeemer" (Isa. 54:8).

This sounds wonderful when it is applied to us, but it sounds like God could be a pushover as a judge when it comes to our enemies. We like mercy for ourselves and justice for others. To be merciful and just is a tricky combination. If you think about it without divine guidance, you will begin to think that mercy is unjust and justice is unmerciful.

The cross ultimately solves this dilemma. The reason God extends such mercy and patience is because his anger with our rebellion is ultimately poured out on Jesus. Make no mistake: the cross is about love *and* anger. God is angrier than any of his creatures, and the cross is where his anger and wrath were fully concentrated. When we turn to Jesus, God's anger is turned away from us and turned toward the cross. His justice is fully satisfied by the very costly price of his Son's death. Meanwhile, his mercy and love are fully expressed to us as he gives us true life through Jesus' death and resurrection.

This liberation from judgment frees us to live for the One who died for us. Having glimpsed the penalty we deserved *and* the love we received, how could we want anything else? So we look to Jesus, who is now both our redeemer and the one we are privileged to imitate and follow. We observe the radical way he handled personal injustice. Jesus *never* was angry because of what was done to him. Instead, he taught us to bless our enemies (Luke 6:27-31). He was only angry when leaders led others down a destructive path or money-changers shamed his

Father's temple. His secret was that he was passionate about his Father's glory, not his own. He completely trusted his Father's judgments to be good and true. He chose to give up his status as judge and entrusted it solely to his Father.

> When they hurled their insults at him, he did not retaliate; when he suffered, he made no threats. Instead, he entrusted himself to him who judges justly. (1 Peter 2:23)

Anger is always a form of imitation. Either we are imitating the way mercy trumps anger in the character of Jesus, or we are mimicking the destructive anger of Satan (John 8:44). There are no other choices.

Looking at Ourselves

Having turned to God to know him better, consider your own heart again. Your task is to judge yourself before you judge others.

> "Why do you look at the speck of sawdust in your brother's eye and pay no attention to the plank in your own eye? How can you say to your brother, 'Let me take the speck out of your eye,' when all the time there is a plank in your own eye? You hypocrite, first take the plank out of your own eye, and then you will see clearly to remove the speck from your brother's eye." (Matt. 7:3-5)

Look at yourself earlier, longer, and harder than you do other people.

This is hard any time, but anger makes it even more difficult because there really may have been an injustice. With anger, finger-pointing is natural. We are absolutely persuaded that what happened is wrong and we are right. But think about the nature of anger. Anger *always* thinks it is right, but it is almost always wrong. Isn't it true that the vast majority of anger is destructive and hurtful? And isn't it true that self-seeking anger will ultimately bring misery on the angry person because anger is contrary to the way God intended us to be?

Ask yourself, "What do I love?" Or, "What rights of mine have been violated?" Personal respect, appreciation, admiration, control, power, impact, being right, revenge, comfort, privacy? If your anger has lasted more than ten minutes, you will find that your own heart is not innocent.

Now connect this to your relationship with God. Your worst relationship with other people reveals your heart before God. If we don't love others, we don't love God. If we are angry with others, we are standing against God. With our complaining and grumbling, we have set up an implicit test for God: Will he give us what we want or not? We have made life about us, and when we do, we are doomed to a life of perpetual dissatisfaction.

Notice the spiritual warfare that rages under the surface. You are listening to diabolic voices that question God's love and power. You don't believe that he will love you well or use his power to judge on your behalf. Wherever we find anger that isn't handled quickly, we will find Satan masterminding division (Eph. 4:26-27).

God responds to us in a very different way than we respond to others. "You, O LORD, are a compassionate and gracious God, slow to anger, abounding in love and faithfulness" (Ps. 86:15). He calls murderers to lead his church as a way to demonstrate his "unlimited patience" to those who believe in him (1 Tim. 1:16). He washes the feet of disciples who betray and reject him (John 13). And he delights in forgiving us, because his forgiveness demonstrates that he is truly the Holy God who doesn't treat us as we deserve.

Trust and Obey

To angry people, God says, "Confess your selfish anger; trust me and obey." Jesus told a story about a man who was forgiven a great debt – more than a lifetime's worth of wages. As soon as he was released from the debt, he tracked down a man who owed him the equivalent of a couple of dollars and demanded immediate payment (Matt. 18:21-35). When the king heard about it, the ungrateful man's injustice so angered him that he withdrew his forgiveness and threw the man in prison. If the man's actions make *you* angry, realize that Jesus is also warning you – "This is how my heavenly Father will treat each of you unless you forgive your brother from your heart." Through Jesus, we have been forgiven for many lifetimes' worth of debt against our Heavenly Father, yet we want those who slight us to pay up immediately.

When that story fits (and it fits us all at some time), it shows that we don't truly grasp God's grace and mercy to us through Christ. We treat others the way we think we have been treated. If we think God has been stingy with us, we will be stingy toward others. But there is another way. Those who know that they have been forgiven will be generous, eager to imitate Christ by covering the offenses of others (Prov. 19:11).

If there has been a serious offense, Scripture is very practical. Talk to the offending person with love. If he doesn't listen, ask others for help to reconcile (Matt. 18:15-16). Certainly, love will take different forms in different relationships, and it is always wise to get advice on how to love, but the goal remains love.

Live like a person who has been released from a huge debt. Or go one step further: live as though you owe others, not as though they owe you (Rom. 13:8).

Response

Anger is one reason why people hold onto depression.

> When I'm depressed, pain is my friend. I wallow in pain. It's what I am familiar with. I'll tell you that I hate my pain and that there is nothing good about it, but I still hold onto it. I'm so dead inside, so empty of any enthusiasm or hope. My pain reminds me that I'm alive. It allows me to be angry.[1]

Remember that anger is devious and hard to find. You can be "doing" anger without even feeling it. Pray, "Lord, search me."

Since prayer is one of the places our heart is revealed, allow it to test you. If you can meditate on the Lord's Prayer (Matt. 6:9-13) and make it your own, it is evidence that you are putting up a good fight against lingering anger.

For a succinct passage of Scripture that summarizes what has been written here (and more), read James 4. Notice that it teaches us to say, "If it is the Lord's will." How many times have you had huge expectations, only to have them dashed on the rocks? How different would it have been if you had begun by saying, "If it is the Lord's will"?

Where do you see anger in your life?

---

[1] Julia Thorne, *You Are Not Alone* (New York: Harper, 1993), p. 30.

CHAPTER 17

Dashed Hopes

Hope is risky. The more you look forward to something, the greater the chance of being let down. Set your heart on a sun-soaked day at the beach and an afternoon shower is very disappointing. It seems safer to take the more pessimistic route and anticipate a monsoon. Then, at least, your hopes won't be dashed.

No doubt you have had your hopes rise and fall in your life. We all have, and it always hurts. "Hope deferred makes the heart sick" (Prov. 13:12). For some people, when dreams crash, they just dream something new. Others, however, at some point decide that they have had enough. They decide never to hope again.

Everyone who goes through suffering should be alert to hopelessness and consider God's response to it. With depression, where hopelessness tends to be so prominent, this is critical.

We Are People Who Hope
Hope is distinctly human. Regardless of how difficult your

life has been, you can remember when you had hopes and dreams. You looked forward to the future. Children anticipate a favorite dessert, a special trip, a birthday party. Teens hope for school vacations, weekends, and times with friends.

In business they call it vision – the ability to think about things that don't yet exist. Experts say this is essential for leadership. More popularly, we call it imagination. Our language is rich with words about hope: wish, yearning, dream, anticipation, desire, eagerness, expectation, goal, ambition, aim, target.

We live in the present. The past can weigh us down, but the future pulls us along. There is a destination to life. We live a story that has a past, present, and future.

To live without hope is to live without a future. It is *almost* impossible to imagine such a life. Cynics and pessimists, however, mock hope, as if we can live without it. Those who are depressed try to kill it because it has betrayed them.

Killing Hope and More

Have you ever made a decision to no longer hope? Some people can remember the exact moment. For others, hope just gradually erodes as disappointments mount. Either way, you feel that hope has given you as much pain as you can handle. It makes sense to either kill it or let it die of natural causes. Only a fool, you think, would continue to hope when so many dreams have proved unattainable.

What you don't realize is that so much of what we associate with life itself is bound up with hope. Hope is the future that reaches into the present. When you see nothing ahead of you in the future, there is no reason to get out of bed, love, or work now. Kill hope and you kill more than you anticipated. You thought it would make life less painful, but all attempts to kill hope kill both future hopes and present joys. If you want to be freed of all disappointments in the future, you have to be unaffected now because what if, in the future, you lose the things you love? Do you have a spouse that you love? A child? The only way to keep safe is to be detached.

If you kill hope, you think you are protecting yourself, but, instead, you doom yourself to lifelessness. If you let hope gradually die without putting up a fight, you end up in the same place. It renders the present meaningless. Without hope, you feel like the walking dead.

If you have a commitment to hopelessness or a reluctance to fight against it, it is killing you. You know that, but you stay the course anyway. Is it momentum? Tradition? Stubbornness? Whatever the reason, there is another way. You must be willing to do battle here.

Dashed Hopes, Anger, and Self-Pity

There is a reason for discussing dashed hopes right after anger. Although disappointments lead to surrender rather than lashing out, anger and hopelessness eventually meet.

Dashed hopes begin with a simple desire. You want something, and what you want is probably a good thing, such as marriage, relationships, a job, health. Gradually the desire gets stronger. It seems attainable. You begin to imagine it. You can almost taste it. And then it vanishes.

When we don't get what we really want, we get frustrated (part of the spectrum of anger). If we can blame it on a person, our response is easier to recognize as anger. But if it feels like circumstances have conspired against us, there is no human face to attach our anger to. As a result, there is no yelling, screaming, or other sign that we readily classify as anger. But if you listen carefully to yourself, you might notice anger in the way that God is less relevant to you. You have marginalized him. You have pushed him away, given him the cold shoulder. You can be indifferent to him. Perhaps you turn toward him for *some* things, but you don't trust him with anything related to your disappointment. This is the cold version of anger.

Look for dashed hopes to be mingled with anger, but realize that they usually don't stop there. Dashed hopes can lead to frustration with God. Frustration with God leads to self-imposed spiritual isolation or withdrawal, and spiritual isolation leads to self-pity.

Jonah

The prophet Jonah illustrates this in his biblical autobiography. As an ancient Israelite, his hope was that Israel would once again reach the heights it had attained under King Solomon, and Israel's enemies would be defeated. Although the kingdom was doing relatively well at the time, other prophets were already prophesying about an exile that would come at the hands of a country from "beyond Damascus" (Amos 5:27). All indicators pointed to Assyria.

Jonah's mission was to go to Assyria and "preach against it, because its wickedness has come up before me" (Jonah 1:2). It seemed like an ideal job that dovetailed with his own dreams: preach judgment against Israel's potential oppressors. But Jonah resisted preaching because he knew that the God of Israel was merciful. Notice the message – the pagan nation was being warned and given an opportunity to change. Then, if the people in the Assyrian city of Nineveh actually repented, which Jonah deemed likely, God would spare them and Jonah's dreams would be in jeopardy.

After a brief but notable detour, Jonah finally preached a bare-bones sermon that, when you read it, sounds unimpressive and unconvincing, but the people responded dramatically. They repented en masse, and God had compassion for them.

Jonah did not get what he wanted. "Jonah was greatly displeased and became angry" (Jonah 4:1). Although the text doesn't state it directly, we know from other Scripture that inappropriate anger, regardless of where it is directed, is ultimately against God. It is saying that God is not good, and that his judgments should be judged rather than trusted.

Jonah then followed a well-worn path. His dashed hopes and anger descended into self-pity. "Now, O Lord, take away my life, for it is better for me to die than to live" (Jonah 4:3). Since Jonah had such a keen sense that God was the giver and taker of life, suicide was out of the question, but he opted for the Old Testament version of it and asked God to take his life. God had not given him what he wanted, so he was angry and hopeless.

"Have you any right to be angry?" was all that God said. Jonah ignored the question.

The next day, while Jonah was sitting outside the city limits, hoping against hope to see fire rain on Nineveh, the Lord shaded him with a vine and then withered it. Now Jonah was even angrier. He wanted shade and God did not give him what he wanted.

"It would be better for me to die than live," Jonah said, to no one in particular.

"Do you have a right to be angry about the vine?" God asked.

"I do," he said. "I am angry enough to die" (Jonah 4:8-9).

There it is: the triad of unmet expectations, anger and self-pity. When they persist, they lead to thoughts of death.

Jonah's Words to Us

We can assume that Jonah wrote this story, which is astounding because he is willing to make himself look so bad. It was one thing to run from God's call to preach to Nineveh. It was spiritually incorrect but politically correct. He could be interpreted as a patriot. But it was quite another to reveal his self-pity, which is never attractive and is even worse in print. He clearly wants us to learn from him.

God is big. God's greatness is on display in this short book. Prior to Jonah, God was certainly greater than all other gods, but this is the first official missionary journey outside Israel's borders. God is announcing that he is also the God of the Gentiles. In other words, God is much bigger than anyone thought. He is the God over the world, not just a particular people.

Have you ever had a sense of peace when you witnessed majestic mountain peaks or ocean expanses? If so, you bear testimony to how we are blessed when we encounter something bigger than ourselves. Our own burdens seem a little lighter when we witness the awesome and the majestic. Such bigness, of course, points to the Creator who is bigger than his creation. Jonah is revealing to us the God who is bigger than we think, and that is just the medicine we need to take us out of ourselves.

God is good. The character of God has infinite facets. "God is a Spirit, infinite, eternal, and unchangeable, in his being, wisdom, power, holiness, and truth."[1] Of these and many other attributes, Scripture often emphasizes that God is great and good, powerful and loving. In Jonah's book, these qualities are on display. The crux of the book is Jonah's defense. "I knew that you are a gracious and compassionate God, slow to anger and abounding in love, a God who relents from sending calamity" (Jonah 4:2). The problem is that this knowledge didn't make a difference. If anything, it made things worse, at least

---

[1] *Westminster Confession of Faith, Shorter Catechism,* Question 4.

from Jonah's perspective.

Odd, given Jonah's confidence in God's love, that he would avoid trusting him. Didn't he believe that God was also merciful to Israel? But his experience matches our own. We might believe that God loves us, but we aren't so sure he will give us what we want. We want to be loved, and we also want to dictate the *way* and by whom we are loved. Jonah believed that God was gracious and compassionate, but he wanted love served up as judgment and destruction against his enemies.

Confession is once again the way out. With Jonah and ourselves, when our desires depart from God's, they become idolatrous. We don't want anything to get between us and our object of worship. Jonah didn't want to submit to God; he wanted to *be* a god.

Confession is when we acknowledge the against-God root of our behaviors. It is the beginning of a process where we turn away from our self-focused desires and turn to the Holy God. When we turn, we realize that we had a very small view of his love. In Jonah's case, he believed that God was good, but he didn't *really* believe it. He believed that his own plans were better. His myopic vision of God's love was such that he believed that if God was good to one nation, he couldn't bless another. He didn't understand that God could be good to both Nineveh and Jerusalem.

Perhaps you agree that God is good. You know what Christ has done, and you believe that the cross is evidence of God's goodness. But his goodness doesn't make a difference to you. It is irrelevant because good is defined on your terms rather than God's. Like a child, the satisfaction of your plans, your wants, and your desires is the standard for God's goodness. Jonah tells us that good must defined by God's terms, not our own. Otherwise, we are standing in judgment of God.

Do you have a right to be angry? Jonah is a very personal book. God is not simply telling him what to say to Nineveh, he is having an actual dialogue with Jonah. These conversations are special events in the Old Testament, so you listen closely when you come across them.

There are three sections to the Lord's words. First, he gives Jonah the message to speak. Then he twice asks Jonah if he has a right to be angry. He concludes by defending his concern for the people of Nineveh. Notice, in particular, the questions God asks. Jonah has run away from God and now is filled with anger and self-pity because God was merciful. In spite of his recalcitrance, God patiently asks Jonah this question when Jonah asks that his life be taken: "Do you have a right to be angry?"

Try it. When you feel like everything is going against you and suicide seems attractive, ask yourself that question: *Do I have a right to be angry?* When you feel like God has taken away your dreams and hopes, ask, *Do I have a right to be angry?* When you can identify your frustration and are tempted to say, *Yes, I have a right to be angry,* let God reason with you about his love. Let him persuade you to say "no" and to trust him.

Selective Optimism

Underneath depression's veil of passivity is a heart that is busy making choices. Sometimes you prefer hopelessness. You want it. You aspire to it. Isn't that a reasonable way to explain why you are so immune to encouragement? You hear the words and understand them, but you don't want them. Even though self-pity and your attempts to kill hope are not working well, you are loyal to your hope-killing strategy.

In response, God speaks words of mercy and grace, even though you don't trust him. Then he repeats them. He pursues you and makes promises to you rather than ask you to make promises to him.

Here are some things about which you can be very optimistic.

He will never leave you. (Heb. 13:5)

He will never put you in a situation where a sinful response is the only way out. (1 Cor. 10:13)

He will give you more and more grace in your battle with sin (Phil. 1:6). You can be optimistic that next week you will love more than you do now.

He will easily be found by those who seek him. He is even found by those who *don't* seek him. (Rom. 10:20)

He will make you fruitful as you abide in him. (John 15:8)

His purposes will never be thwarted. (Eph. 1:11)

God always says "yes" to these promises.

Good and Very Good

Depression is right when it says that death and sin cast a shadow over everything. There is reason to feel misery. But depression is wrong in surrendering to this interpretation. It is not the entire story. King Jesus has returned and is establishing his reign. The kingdom broke through with great power when the Holy Spirit was given and it continues to grow (Mark 4:30-32).

Depression, therefore, sees some things accurately but is absolutely blind to others. It misses how the Spirit of the Living God is on the move right now, right in front of you.

On this side of the cross, misery persists but the scales are tipped in favor of joy. The King is seated; the celebration has begun in heaven; we could not be loved any more than we are right now; and there are tastes of heaven available even now. There are realities present now that can sustain your hopes.

Pray for eyes to see.

Response

Whether you have killed hope or never nurtured it, hopelessness is lethal. You have already heard the question, "Do you want to change?" Now you understand why such a question is important. There are logical reasons to resist change. For example, what if hope creeps in? You might want to feel less miserable but not at the expense of awakening hope. Jonah certainly didn't want to change, at least not at first. Most likely, you want to change less than you realize. So don't be deceived. We *do* hopelessness. We choose it. But there is a way out.

Part of the answer goes back to what God says to people who fear. The connection is that fear, like hopelessness, is reluctant to trust God for the future. God says that he will give you grace to handle the disappointments that lie ahead; your task is to live for him in the present. At first, this feels reckless, as if you were enjoying the thrill of a speeding car when you are courting devastation at the next turn. But it isn't reckless to trust in God rather than yourself.

Therefore, to fight against hopelessness is to take action in the present. You think that checking off a to-do list is unspiritual? When done by faith, it is heroic.

There are paradoxes in depression; there are also apparent paradoxes in the way God works in us. For example, if you want vitality in the present, entrust your future to the Lord. If you want to have glimpses of hope for tomorrow, trust God now.

What are your dashed hopes? What have you done with them? Where are your new, emerging hopes?

CHAPTER 18

Failure and Shame

Dashed hopes come when we want something and don't get it. For example, you dreamed about financial security by the time you were forty, but you are still living hand-to-mouth. Although you worked hard, a poor economy conspired against you. Or you dreamed of the ideal marriage, but you are starting to believe that there *is* no Mr. Right. It always seemed as though the wrong person was interested in you and the right person was interested in someone else.

Notice that we can't always achieve our hopes on our own. The desired object is never fully in our grasp. We need some help to attain it. For that reason, we don't immediately blame ourselves for these disappointments because we can't control the outcome.

Failure and shame, however, are different. They point the finger at you more than outside circumstances. *You* have not measured up to your own expectations or the expectations of others. You can even see it in your posture. It is as if the unmet expectations and standards weigh you down. You can almost feel them; you half expect them to register on the bathroom scales. The weight is all on you. There is no one else to blame.

175

Chapter Eighteen

Whose Standards?

Depression travels hand in hand with low self-worth. It is even part of the American Psychiatric Association's definition of depression. This sense of worthlessness touches everything you do; it even extends to who you are. (In fact, if you are *not* experiencing low self-worth, you might be experiencing a medical problem than mimics depression.)

Human beings evaluate worth; there is no question about that. We make judgments about people, music, art and hundreds of other events in a normal day. They are good or bad, valuable or expendable, right or wrong. So it is no surprise that we also make evaluations or judgments about ourselves. According to some standard, we determine that we have not measured up.

Whose standard? It varies, but the emotional consequences are the same. You feel miserable and keep veering off into self-loathing.

The standard may be old parental expectations that were communicated through daily criticism, unpredictable punishment or parental indifference.

The standard may be cultural expectations of success and failure that become apparent when you receive an invitation to a high school reunion.

The standard may be God's unwavering commandments.

Whatever the standard, we have failed. As a result, low self-worth is evident in everyone. You will find it in the wealthy physician, the professional athlete, the runway model, and the movie star. The self-judgments of the depressed just tend to be louder.

The way out seems clear: we reject the standards imposed by other people; we don't worry much about God's commandments because no one measures up to them anyway; and we reassess ourselves with standards that are less oppressive, more balanced and fair. Like all people, you are a hybrid of good and bad, strengths and weaknesses. If you are going to evaluate the bad, learn to include the good. This would hopefully keep your self-image on an even keel.

The problem, of course, is that it is not this easy. Even if you could find some strengths and some good within yourself – which is almost impossible when you are depressed – they don't seem like enough to counter-balance everything that makes you feel so worthless. People who care about you have already affirmed you, and it hasn't made any difference. There is a deeper problem that must be confronted.

Reorient yourself by recalling the nature of the human heart. Many problems come at us, but they don't just encounter a blank interior. They are interpreted by hearts that are constantly busy. When depressed, we feel like an empty shell, but we are doing something. Remember, the heart is always choosing.

Try reframing your experience with this in mind. For example, instead of thinking that you are oppressed by the expectations that others have draped over you, recognize that the heart *chooses* to live under the standards of others. Instead of thinking that you are distressed because people aren't pleased with you, recognize that you have chosen a style of life in which you live for approval. We don't want to experience failure and shame; we don't choose that. But we *do* choose to trust in other people and their judgments. It comes down once again to the deepest question of all: who will you trust?

Scripture indicates that we come from a long line of incorrigible idolaters. Long ago it was Baal, but Baal was never the favorite idol. The true favorites have always been money and people. These two continue to be the most popular objects of worship. Why do we choose these idols? Because we think they can satisfy. We think they can give us what we want.

Let's apply this to depression. We want admiration, respect, honor, influence, kindness, or love. We could buy it, but we still need people to give us what we want. So we live based on their expectations, opinions, and standards. Other people become our gods. Our purpose, of course, is not to be subservient to them. Our goal is to receive what we want by appeasing them. Give them what they want and they will give you what you need.

But the devil is in the details. The fine print in this arrangement promises two things. First, other people will never satisfy. You can never measure up well enough, and you can never get enough of what you want from them. Second, you become a servant to whatever you trust in. If you trust in money, you will slavishly try to get it and worry when you can't. If you trust in people, your life will be devoted to meeting their expectations.

This isn't to say that wanting respect, love and other things we get from relationships is wrong. Idolatry is usually a good thing that has gone haywire. You can tell that something has gone wrong when you move from the goal of God's glory to your own. Remember, we want to make it about us, but it's not.

Sometimes it is hard to detect the gradual deification of people in our lives. Our hearts erect the pedestals for these idols while our backs are turned, but there is a way to alert yourself to what's going on. When you are lukewarm toward God, or when you are not fixing your eyes on Jesus, then you can be sure that idolatry has taken root. If you are not worshiping the true God, you are worshiping something else.

An even easier strategy is just to *assume* that you erect idols. Our hearts can believe the right things but still be double-minded. Like Aaron and Israel when they were waiting for Moses, they believed that the true God had delivered them from

Egypt, but they also built a golden calf.

People-gods

If failure and shame fit your experience, then you most likely have people-gods. You want something from them and they haven't delivered. Depression doesn't exempt you from the problems that afflict us all, and all of us have an instinct that turns us away from God and towards people.

At first, the isolation of depression suggests that we are distanced from and unmoved by other people. But other people play a huge part in our self-judgments. A person truly isolated – marooned on a deserted island – does not have to negotiate through shame and failure. There are no people recounting personal failures, and there simply isn't anyone around to trust. But you don't live on a deserted island. You may try to psychologically escape to one, but people are still around, and their presence reminds you that you don't measure up. On top of that, no matter where you try to flee, your own heart goes with you. You can't escape that with a change in geography.

Low self-worth and a sense of failure and shame do not simply arise because we feel bad about ourselves. We have also trusted in other people, and we think that *they* feel bad about us. Perhaps we have experienced overt rejection from someone especially important to us, but the truth is that we don't really need anyone to speak against us. *We* can tell when we have failed. We know people who do it better than we do, are more attractive than we are, seem to have more intimate relationships, better jobs, and so on. It is as if we are born with an innate ability to poll the world on hundreds of different measures, and on the ones most important to us, we rate average or worse. We fear that we are ordinary.

Toppling Idols

You realize, of course, that when we talk about trusting in anything or anyone other than God, we are talking about sin. Please don't run away from that. Sin has been given a bad name by those who stand in hypocritical judgment of others. The reality is that the Spirit himself is the one who convicts us of sin. God is pleased when we see sin and confess it.

One of the blessings of seeing sin is that we can actually do something about it. We can call out for mercy, find it, and change. The Spirit has been given so that we no longer have to be slaves to sin. There is a way out.

When in doubt, the way out is to get back to basic purpose statements. "I belong to God. The way I can honor, please and glorify him is by trusting him and responding to him with obedience." Love God, love neighbor. Trust and obey. In God's good plan, he has determined that these ordinary spiritual acts would be the pinnacle of true humanness.

Trust. When we put our trust in the judgments of others, we are saying something to God. We are saying, "I don't trust you." "You are not enough." You believe that God offers you heaven, but can he satisfy your ever-growing psychological desires? Can he make you an "A," at least in some areas, when you feel like a "C-minus"?

But that's missing the point. Our purpose is not about us, it is about God. For this reason, God seems to prefer the average and below average. Otherwise it would be about our talents and abilities.

> Brothers, think of what you were when you were called. Not many of you were wise by human standards; not many were influential; not many were of noble birth. But God chose the foolish things of

the world to shame the wise; God chose the weak things of the world to shame the strong. He chose the lowly things of this world and the despised things . . . "Let him who boasts boast in the Lord." (1 Cor. 1:26-28, 31)

When I am weak, then I am strong. (2 Cor. 12:10)

"Let not the wise man boast of his wisdom or the strong man boast of his strength or the rich man boast of his riches, but let him who boasts boast about this: that he understands and knows me, that I am the LORD, who exercises kindness, justice and righteousness on earth, for in these I delight," declares the LORD. (Jer. 9:23-24)

Life is not about my resumé, it is about ways to extend the fame of Jesus. And one way to do this is to say that God is more than enough. After all, he *is* love. It has been proven at the cross. All other loves are, at best, imitations that point back to the original rather than usurp it.

To trust is to say that we need Jesus. Our search for self-satisfaction has been a failure, and we now turn to the One who, all along, has been our true destination.

There is a certain paradox in trusting God. When we trust him, we are saying that we are entirely inadequate, which is true though it doesn't do wonders for our self-image. But when we trust him, it is also as if we have arrived home. All is well. Yes, there may be many problems, but we are home, and the comfort and joy of home reduces the problems of life to the level of hassles. We have the Father's love, and we know that he is the ruling king. That is enough.

Confess. As you turn back to the Lord, speak your confession to him. Tell him that your heart is prone to wander, your tendencies toward erecting idols incorrigible. Confession is speaking the truth about our hearts to the Lord. Although Scripture encourages us to make it a daily feature of our conversations with God (Matt. 6:9-13), it is a neglected discipline.

A rule of thumb in confession is to keep at it until you have inklings of hope or joy. Confession is not a time to grovel. It is a time to trust in the God who delights in forgiving because it brings him glory. Don't forget the story of the joy the shepherd takes in the one lost sheep that is found.

> If a man owns a hundred sheep, and one of them wanders away, will he not leave the ninety-nine on the hills and go to look for the one that wandered off? And if he finds it, I tell you the truth, he is happier about that one sheep than about the ninety-nine that did not wander off. In the same way your Father in heaven is not willing that any of these little ones should be lost. (Matt. 18:12-14)

Yes, you wander off, but focus on the happiness of the shepherd. It isn't what you expected.

Obey. Our response to God's love is summarized as loving our neighbors. This simple expression of obedience is a profound treatment for failure and shame. At first it seems counterintuitive. After all, our problem was that we fell in love with what we could receive from others; it would make more sense to detach from them. This love, however, is different. It is the love of a person freed rather than enslaved. Having received the love of Christ, we are willing to say to other people,

"My desire to love you will outweigh my desire to be loved [honored, appreciated, respected] by you."

Can you imagine the freedom in this? No longer are we dominated by popular opinion. Perceived rejection doesn't control us as it once did. Instead, we keep coming back to the question, "What form will love take now?"

Response

Notice the connection to anger. If anger is a judgment we make about others, low self-worth seems to be a judgment we make about ourselves. We say, "*I* am wrong. *I* deserve blame." The tie to anger is even more apparent when we rename low self-esteem as self-hatred or self-loathing.

When you turn to Christ, these judgments become less important. You don't have to say, "I am special because God loves me," which is true but not the critical issue. And you don't have to say, "What a miserable, idolatrous wretch," which is also true but also not the critical issue. Instead, you simply think less often about yourself. Your successes and failures are still noticeable, but they don't encumber you the way they once did.

CHAPTER 19

Guilt and Legalism

Failure and shame are signposts. It seems as if they only relate to ourselves or our relationships with other people, but they really point to a deeper sense of not being OK before God. The principle is this: if you see a problem in your relationships with other people, you will find the identical problem in your relationship with God. If you are angry with others, you will find anger with God. If you don't love others, you don't love God. If you feel as if you can't measure up to the expectations of yourself and others, then you feel as if you have not measured up to God's standards either. What we call failure, shame, and not measuring up before other people, we call guilt before God.

To understand this, you have to remember that we are not always aware of the things that influence us. At this moment there are thousands of people who have somehow contributed to your life. They have affected your present emotions, thoughts, and dreams, but you are not aware of them. It should come as no surprise that the Living God, before whose face we always live, has an impact on us whether we are consciously

185

thinking about him or not.

Where Is Guilt?

"Laura has gained so much weight – she looks terrible!"

When you say this to someone other than Laura, you don't feel guilty. But what if Laura overhears? You will either never want to see Laura again or apologize endlessly. Why is it that you were oblivious to your wrongdoing one moment and ashamed of it the next? The difference, of course, is the presence of Laura.

Scripture teaches that we all know God, but we try to keep that knowledge at bay. For those who successfully suppress that knowledge, God seems very far away. Guilt, too, is a distant memory. For the rest of us, however, in whom the knowledge of God continues to impress itself, guilt is palpable and it affects us more than we think. And that is a good sign – it is a gift! It means that God is on the move in your life, giving you grace to see sin and change instead of being blind to it.

If you can't immediately find guilt in your life, here are some questions that may bring it to the surface:

> If you saw God face to face today, is there anything you would be ashamed of?
>
> If all your private thoughts were advertised, would you want to hide?
>
> What would it be like if you were certain that you were forgiven for all your sins? Would life feel any different to you?
>
> What would it be like if you knew that your Heavenly Father accepted you with enthusiasm?

The only time anyone ever talks about guilt is during a Sunday sermon. It is not part of our normal discussions. We are not accustomed to looking for it. But be patient; you will find it.

Varieties of Guilt

There are a number of reasons why we can feel guilty.

1. We feel guilty because we *should* feel guilty. We love sin more than God and we plan to keep on sinning. Occasionally, we throw in the "I'm only human" rationale.

2. We feel guilty because we don't confess our sin to God.

    > Then I acknowledged my sin to you, and did not cover up my iniquity. I said, "I will confess my transgressions to the LORD" – and you forgave the guilt of my sin. (Ps. 32:5)

3. We feel guilty because there are still consequences to past sin. For example, a family member was severely injured by your drunk driving, and you see that person every day. Assuming that there has been confession and appropriate restitution, this is more accurately sadness than it is guilt before God.

4. We feel guilty, but what we are really feeling is a sense of uncleanness because we have been victimized by someone else. Sometimes the experience of being unclean from our own sin and being unclean from the sin of others is hard to distinguish. They are, however, very different.

5. We feel guilty because we think we must do something to be forgiven.

This last type of guilt is especially relevant to depression.

The Gospel

The story of the cross is also called the gospel, which simply means that it is good news. What makes it good news is that there is forgiveness of sins. It is given through faith in Jesus rather than through our own good works. That is why you have heard the call to trust over and over. If our lives are going to have any bedrock, it will be our faith or trust in what God has done through Jesus.

> I am not ashamed of the gospel, because it is the power of God for the salvation of everyone who believes . . . For in the gospel a righteousness from God is revealed, a righteousness that is by faith from first to last. (Rom. 1:16-17)

> "In repentance and rest is your salvation, in quietness and trust is your strength." (Isa. 30:15)

All of this is unmistakably divine. No one could invent such a one-sided arrangement. We sin against God – that is what we bring to the table. God pursues us, sends his Son to suffer the death penalty, adopts us, gives us the righteousness of Jesus, changes us to look more and more like him, and loves us through eternity. He simply tells us to trust in him rather than in ourselves.

Legalism: The Anti-Gospel

You would think that once we heard this good news, we would embrace it with all our hearts. We have found the pearl of great price. We have been given the greatest and most costly gift, and the Giver delights in giving it because of his love for us. Eureka! This is the treasure we have been waiting for. Everything else we pursued and temporarily adored was a mere counterfeit of this amazing gift. Considering what we have received, we could never pursue them again.

This is what you would *think* our response would be, but there are times we surprise even ourselves. For some reason, we like the old arrangement where we have to try to make it on our own. Perhaps the notion that we can't bring anything to the table is too humbling for us. After all, only a child acknowledges being needy, and that is what the gospel requires us to do. We are required to say, "I need Jesus." So we lobby for something other than the gospel.

This anti-gospel is called legalism, works righteousness, or living under the law. It simply means that we trust in Christ *and* something we do. In the New Testament, circumcision was the deed that was added. Today we have dropped circumcision but our creative alternatives know no bounds. We have added hundreds of other activities, some of which can sound quite pious. For example, in medieval times, people would whip themselves to show their sorrow for sin. Today, anorectics starve themselves; others just stagger in self-loathing.

It sounds religious and contrite until you really think about it. Then you realize that when you add *anything* to what Christ has done, it diminishes the glory of God. It is a rejection of God's gift as sufficient. We can try to excuse ourselves and say that the gospel seems too good to be true. But no matter what we say, when we add something to the gospel we are minimizing the completeness of God's work, and we are essentially trying to share the glory with God by bringing our own gift.

Finding Legalism

Legalism is more common than you think. It is another one of those human instincts that you will find lodged in every heart.

> Have you ever said, "I just can't forgive myself"?
> Is your life one long, "If only . . ."?
> Have others called you driven?
> Are you burdened by past sins?
> Do you believe that God is chronically disappointed in you?
> Do you believe that God likes you more when you are really good?
> Do you make deals with God: "If you . . . I will . . ."?

Can you hear within these questions the conviction that your relationship with God rests more with you than with him?

Now consider what you might add to the gospel. Life is found in God + _____.

> Serving in church
> Reading my Bible
> Not being too mean
> Being relatively honest
> Not getting drunk
> Being sexually careful

Notice that these are good things. What makes them ugly are the motives that drive them. If you do these things to find favor before God, they are worthless. When they become activities in which we trust, they are abominations because they replace God.

We make these additions to the gospel because they allow us to feel good about ourselves *apart* from God. They also give us a basis for judging others. If we have successfully gone through a day and measured up to our new law, we are a success (however temporarily). And we are now entitled to judge others who don't measure up.

Even God himself doesn't escape our judgment. "I have been a good daughter even though I have had to live with a messed-up father. Why is God doing this to me?" If we have done the right thing, we feel we have a right to get something in return, and we can become angry or depressed when we don't get it.

With this in mind, add some other signs of legalism.

"After all I have done, this is the thanks I get?"
"Life isn't fair."

There are small, short-lived payoffs to legalism, but the emotional cornerstone of legalism is a lack of joy (Gal. 4:15). Could you expect anything else? If you believe that your most important relationship is dependent on appeasing an angry or irritated God, no matter how much you do, you will never be sure it is enough.

In reality, whatever good deeds we do are intended to be a *response* to what God has done, not a cause of it. God's grace and love to us *precede* our own good works. He loved us before we loved him or even acknowledged him. Given this fact, why do we now think that we can earn his approval?

Jane had an abortion ten years ago and has been depressed ever since. She still feels guilty about what she has done. Her friends have been faithful in loving her and speaking about forgiveness of sins, and she knows the truth of the cross, but it doesn't seem to matter. It is as if her guilt is a resistant virus that is immune to the gospel.

Legalism explains Jane's distress. She has all the earmarks of following the anti-gospel. If the gospel she believed was Christ alone, her sorrow over sin would be increasingly displaced by thankfulness. But to Jane, the gospel doesn't even seem relevant. And when the gospel isn't relevant, the anti-gospel has taken its place. Her anti-gospel is that life and forgiveness come through Christ *plus* not having an abortion.

Having violated her beliefs and standards, she "had to" be punished. She could not reverse the consequences of her abortion, so she decided that her self-imposed punishment would be grief, and it would be long and severe. Perhaps, after an unspecified period of suffering, she would allow herself to be forgiven.

But how severe must her penance be? And how long? Multiple suicide attempts and daily reflection on her past actions were not judged to be enough. So she continued in her grief, hoping that one day she would wake up and find that her penance had finally satisfied God's justice.

Turning Back

"Tell me, you who want to be under the law," wrote Paul to the church. The gospel becomes a new self-imposed law when we add anything to what Christ has done, and Paul says that we actually prefer this arrangement.

Leaving entrenched legalism is a straightforward process, but you should expect to leave many times. It won't happen all at once. In Paul's book to the churches in Galatia, he marshals a number of arguments to persuade people of the truth of Christ and the error of legalism.

- He expresses his personal astonishment that people would turn from the grace of Christ (Gal. 1:6).

- He establishes his own credentials to speak with authority (Gal. 1:11-2:14).
- He cites Abraham as an example of how we are first given promises we receive by faith, and only then are we given rules for living. These are responses to this grace (Gal. 3:1-25).
- He cites how God chose Isaac, Abraham's son by God's promise, rather than Ishmael, Abraham's son by a man-made plan (Gal. 4:21-31).
- He reminds us that it is only grace that keeps us from racism and other forms of pride. Otherwise, we judge by laws we think we have kept and others have not. If we add our works to the grace of God, we will no longer be one people unified by Christ, but one small clique that thinks it is better than the others (Gal. 3:26-29).
- He keeps emphasizing that he wants us to be free, and freedom can only be found when we acknowledge that Christ has done it all (Gal. 5:1-5).

Paul summarizes his teaching against legalism with this familiar exhortation: "The only thing that counts is faith expressing itself through love" (Gal. 5:6). If this is true (and it is) we as legalists should respond by saying, "Lord, forgive me." We had been counting on something we could accomplish ourselves rather than relying on the grace of God. We were actually proud enough to think we could please God on our own merits. To think so, we must have had a very superficial understanding of sin.

Jane felt guilty because she had an abortion, but what about the unbelief and other sins she commits daily? While she was maximizing the sin of abortion, placing it beyond the scope of forgiveness and punishing herself instead, she was minimizing all of her other sins. She was doing nothing to punish herself for them. If she is going to try to earn favor with God by human effort, she is obligated to keep *all* the law (Gal. 5:3), and that, of course, is impossible.

The only way out is for Jane to say, "Lord, forgive me" – not because of her abortion (she has confessed that thousands of times), but because of her attempts to deal with sin by human effort rather than faith. Then she should stay in the shadow of the cross, remember daily that she stands before God because of his grace and not her effort, and then get on with the wonderful task of loving other people.

Response

In Jane's case, legalism was the cause of her depression. If it is not one of the *causes* of your depression, you can be sure that it will be *revealed* by it. When you see it, be hopeful. You know that you are on the right track when you see your legalism. When it is dealt with, joy is within reach. The people of Galatia were going through severe hardships, but it was their legalism that robbed them of their joy. And it was their returning to the heart of the gospel that recovered their joy.

For another biography, read Philippians 3:4-11. Paul looks back on his life and his many good accomplishments and tells us that he considers them worthless compared to what Christ has given him through faith.

Where do you see your own legalism?

CHAPTER 20

Death

As God's offspring, we desire life. God is the author of life; he says that life is a good thing, and we tacitly agree. You, too, naturally desired life. There was a time when death, at least as an option, was never a thought. It didn't cross your mind. But then there it was.

When it first came, even you were surprised. The thought was so foreign that it seemed to be implanted by someone else. You felt like an observer as it whizzed by. Over time, these shocking thoughts became more common. For some, they remain a terrible nuisance. For others, these thoughts eventually felt comfortable, to the point of feeling natural, good, and right.

If you are depressed, you have a rocky relationship with death. You want it but you fear it. Thankfully, fear and other circumstances keep many people from acting on their impulses, but fear is not a lasting deterrent. A moment's desperation could overrule it. Please take time to think more deeply about your hopelessness.

Chapter Twenty

Suicidal Thinking

There is *some* truth in suicidal thinking. When life is examined apart from God, thoughts of death make perfect sense. The writer of Ecclesiastes saw this; so did Nietzsche when he said that, for all practical purposes, God is dead. When God is dead, there is no purpose, no future. We are dead too.

But suicidal thinking only sees part of the picture. In fact, it *insists* on only seeing part of the picture – the part that will confirm its interpretation of reality. If you have thought about suicide, its logic is clear and simple, but it is irrational.

> You are certain of a catastrophic future. But you have always predicted catastrophes and you have been a woefully inaccurate prophet.
>
> You think that death is the only option, but you forget that there are times when your pain is less severe. And you have forgotten that you have done a number of things that have made your pain more tolerable.
>
> You think that no one would care if you took your own life, but you are blind to the people who have tried to help, and you know that every suicide leaves a wake of mourners whose lives are forever changed.
>
> You think that God doesn't hear or care, but you also believe that his heaven is a pain-free paradise.
>
> You think that you must solve impossible problems, but God calls you to tasks that are smaller and more ordinary. He calls you to look around and be faithful with what is directly in front of you.

You are preoccupied with death. Given that God is life, that fact alone should give you doubts about your reasoning. You might even derive a perverse satisfaction from considering the means of suicide. But having tasted something of hell, you are fearful of death. You are concerned that death would give you the "full blast."[1] "Dread" captures your experience. Like a child watching a scary movie, you shield your eyes but peek through your fingers.

> Dread is a desire for what one fears, a sympathetic antipathy; dread is an alien power which takes hold of an individual, and yet one cannot extricate oneself from it, does not wish to . . . but what one fears attracts one.[2]

The paradoxes continue. You feel more desperate than anyone alive. You feel helpless before the sinkhole of pain. You feel absolutely powerless. But meditations on suicide are the ultimate expression of human autonomy and control. Against all counsel, you persist in thinking about death and suicide. You choose individualism. Self-law. You do what you want. It sounds like a declaration of independence, and it sounds angry.

All you know, however, is that your pain is intolerable. You can't take it any more, and there is no relief in sight. That is enough. Other facts are irrelevant.

Why?

When you are depressed, you rarely challenge your own thinking. When your depression includes suicidal thoughts, you

---

[1] William and Lucy Hulme, *Wrestling with Depression* (Minneapolis: Augsburg, 1995), p.28.

[2] *The Journals of Kierkegaard*, 1834-1854, edited and translated by Alexander Dru (London: Collins, 1958), pp.79-80.

challenge them even less. Yet this is too important to leave unexamined.

You think about death because you can't take the pain any more. Have you considered where the pain is coming from? It rarely comes from nowhere.

Is the pain always this intense or does it fluctuate? What intensifies it? What decreases it? When you are in the most extreme pain, you forget that it doesn't stay at that pitch.

What have you lost that is so precious to you? What do you believe you need that you don't have? You will discover where you have placed your trust with these questions.

What are you afraid to face? Shame has led many people to despair, but God's forgiveness covers both guilt and shame.

Does your pain have anything to do with another person? If so, Scripture is full of hope for asking forgiveness, forgiving, and reconciling.

What do you expect death to do? You want it to take away the pain, but what else? Would it also be a statement to anyone?

Why do you feel powerless? Have you listened to the counsel of others? What have they said? What have you done?

Why, really, don't you want to live?

Who Is God?

The connection between our distress and our relationship with God is not always obvious, but the topic of suicidal thoughts makes the connection unavoidable. Suffering always raises theological questions, but death and suicide compel them. Death is the one place where religion still reigns over all discussions. And, most importantly, death means that you will meet God.

Who is God?

Do you believe he hears? Do you believe that he is the God of great compassion? Do you believe that his compassion is active – that he is doing something now? Do you believe he gives grace to persevere in trials? Do you believe that he knows the details of your pain and gives you enough grace every day? What difference would it make if you did believe these truths?

Do you know that the risen Jesus is "sustaining all things by his powerful word" (Heb. 1:3)?

Have you really tried to know the mind of God regarding your present situation? Who have you spoken with? Has anyone suggested that suicide is a wise choice? What Scripture have you read? How have you prayed?

Do you understand the gospel? The gospel is about the resurrection, and the resurrection is the ground for hope.

If you think suicide is a good or viable option, you don't know God. You think he is silent, but he is not. He is generous in the way he reveals himself, and he speaks clearly. He speaks of his patience and love for you. He calls you to trust him and to let that trust express itself in love toward others. He says he gives you grace to persevere and teaches you how to persevere. Maybe you are listening for something other than what he is saying.

Read the end of Job again (Job 38-42). Job was tortured with physical and psychological pain. He wrestled with issues of life and death more extensively than any human in Scripture. Throughout it all, he persevered in faith but felt like he needed more from God. He wanted to understand more of his ways.

God's response was to emphatically state that he was God. His questions to Job began like this:

> "Brace yourself like a man; I will question you, and you shall answer me.
>
> Where were you when I laid the earth's foundation? Tell me, if you understand.
>
> Who marked off its dimensions? Surely you know! Who stretched a measuring line across it?
>
> On what were its footings set, or who laid its cornerstone – while the morning stars sang together and all the angels shouted for joy?
>
> Who shut up the sea behind doors when it burst forth from the womb, when I made the clouds its garment and wrapped it in thick darkness, when I fixed limits for it and set its doors and bars in place, when I said, 'This far you may come and no farther; here is where your proud waves halt'"? (Job 38:3-11)

Be sure to read all of God's questions. They will allow you to see a much bigger story. They will, at least, take your eyes away from the immensity of your pain and point you to the object of hope.

No More Than You Can Bear?

If you are looking for answers, Job is one of many places you can turn. Another is to God's promises.

> No temptation has seized you except what is common to man. And God is faithful; he will not let you be tempted beyond what you can bear. But when you are tempted, he will also provide a way out so that you can stand up under it. (1 Cor. 10:13)

This is one of the better known promises, and it is one where God appears to have reneged, because severe depression feels like more than you can bear. Therefore, it is important to consider for two reasons. First, it is a great promise. Second, if you are starting to believe that it isn't always true, then you may start asking where else God's promises might have exceptions. Such doubts erode faith.

When you read the larger passage, it recounts Israel's exodus from Egypt and their struggles in the desert. When difficulties came, many of the people quickly abandoned God and either grumbled against him or turned to idols. This passage is saying that you too will go through a desert, and when you do, the Spirit will strengthen you in such a way that you can avoid grumbling and idolatry. God's promise is that he will never put us in a situation where we have no choice but to sin. He either will relieve the intensity of the temptation or he will give us grace to trust and obey in the hardship. This promise means that depression cannot coerce you to sin.

The shrug and indifference that this so often elicits reveals the irrationality within us all. From our perspective, there is only one thing that God could say that would cause us to listen: we want him to take away the pain. From God's perspective, however, the most important thing he could give us is the power to trust and obey when we feel powerless. In the mind of God, sin is a much more serious problem than suffering. In ours, the order is reversed.

Here is a place to start. Consider that your present hopelessness is sin. Either you have put your trust in something other than Christ, which is sin, or, like the Israelites in the desert, you have essentially said that what God says is not true, which is the sin of unbelief.

God not only forgives these sins against him, he empowers you to put your hope in him. In your despair, can you ask God to give you grace to resist sin and trust him through suffering?

What Is Your Only Comfort?

Job opens our eyes to see God's greatness. The promise from 1 Corinthians 10:13 opens our eyes to the fact that our sin is more serious than our suffering. Many other passages open our eyes to the God who comforts his people. The Lord is the good shepherd whose presence comforts the sheep. He is the one who calls out, "Comfort, comfort my people" (Isa. 40:1), and the one who is called "the God of all comfort" (2 Cor. 1:3).

Where is this comfort? Ask for it. Ask to have eyes open to seeing it. Look for it. Ask others to point the way. The comfort you are looking for is available, and it can be found in Jesus Christ.

> *Question 1.* What is your only comfort in life and in death?
> *Answer:* That I belong – body and soul, in life and in death – not to myself but to my faithful Savior, Jesus Christ, who at the cost of his own blood has fully paid for all my sins and has completely freed me from the dominion of the devil; that he protects me so well

that without the will of my Father in heaven not a hair can fall from my head; indeed, that everything must fit his purpose for my salvation. Therefore, by his Holy Spirit, he also assures me of eternal life, and makes me wholeheartedly willing and ready from now on to live unto him.[3]

This comfort comes in two parts: in the knowledge of Jesus, and in the fact that we belong to him through faith.

You don't belong to yourself. That certainly adds purpose, hope, and comfort to life. "You were bought at a price" (1 Cor. 6:20), "not with perishable things such as silver or gold... but with the precious blood of Christ, a lamb without blemish or defect" (1 Peter 1:18-19). "You are of Christ, and Christ is of God" (1 Cor. 3:23).

If you are self-employed and you don't care whether your business succeeds or fails, there is no reason to work. Occasionally, you might get out of bed and go through the motions for the sake of loved ones, but your heart wouldn't be in it. But if you were an ambassador, called by the king – a royal emissary – you wouldn't think about whether or not to get up. You simply get up. You are on a mission.

God, you say, can easily get a replacement. You won't be missed. There are, after all, thousands from which to choose. Be careful on this one. Be suspicious. Lies can mingle with the truth. Of course, God has called many people to himself, and he will accomplish his purposes. The reality, however, is that he chooses people, especially weak people, to accomplish them. He chooses individual people, and has established our tasks from before the foundation of the world (Eph. 2:10). The comfort is that *you* belong to him.

---

[3] *The Heidelberg Catechism* (Cleveland, Ohio: United Church Press, 1962), p. 9.

Response

Can you pray that you would share this song of praise with the apostle Paul?

> Praise be to the God and Father of our Lord Jesus Christ, the Father of compassion and the God of all comfort, who comforts us in all our troubles, so that we can comfort those in any trouble with the comfort we ourselves have received from God. (2 Cor. 1:3-4)

Why do you think about death? What does God say to you when you find hope in suicidal thoughts?

PART THREE   *Other Help and Advice*

CHAPTER 21

Medical Treatments

Depression involves the whole person, body and soul. The soul or heart is always busy interpreting painful circumstances and sorting out basic allegiances. The body just feels sick.

Following Scripture's lead, matters of the heart are the priority.

> Physical training is of some value, but godliness [spiritual training] has value for all things, holding promise for both the present life and the life to come. (1 Tim. 4:8)

The heart is the real battleground during suffering, and it deserves your utmost attention. As you learn how to put your hope in Christ, your work reaps eternal benefits. But that isn't all. Since you are a seamless interconnection of physical and spiritual, your physical body can respond to your spiritual growth, and in depression it usually does. In other words, as the Spirit, Scripture, and wise people guide you, you will probably feel lighter (2 Cor. 4:16-18). Your pain won't have the same devastating power.

Most current thinking tends to miss the spiritual essence of depression. It specializes instead in physical treatments, and they, too, can lighten the physical experience of depression. Antidepressant medications are the best known and most popular of these treatments, but there are hundreds of proposed physical aids, and many of them can change the physical experience of depression. They will not give you hope, but they might make you feel less miserable. Physical treatments are able to change physical symptoms but they are *only* able to change physical symptoms.

Antidepressants

There is broad agreement that antidepressant medication can make some people feel better. In fact, there are times when the reduction in depressive symptoms can be dramatic. That is its major advantage.

But there is much we still don't know. For example, we don't know why it helps. The most popular hypothesis is that depression is related, in part, to a lack of the brain chemical serotonin. Many of the new medications, called serotonin reuptake inhibitors (SSRIs), make this chemical more available in the brain. If these help, that would seem to establish the presence of a specific chemical imbalance. But there are well over fifty neurotransmitters in the brain, they are found over large areas, and their interactions with one another defy present analysis. The truth is that the biological hypotheses rest on shaky ground.

When medication helps, we don't know why. The brain is simply too complex and our knowledge of its mechanics is too primitive. This year, serotonin is the favored neurotransmitter. In previous years it was dopamine. In future years it will be another brain chemical. There remain many unanswered questions.

- We don't know why medication helps some people.
- We don't know why it *doesn't* help others.
- We don't know why, for any individual person, some medications are more effective than others.
- We don't know why medications that are chemically different have similar effects.
- We don't know why antidepressants seem to be equally effective with seemingly unrelated problems, such as obsessive thoughts and compulsive behavior.
- We don't know why it can take up to a month before people notice a difference.
- We don't know why antidepressants often lose their effectiveness over time.

At this point, the most apt analogy for how these medications work is aspirin. Aspirin can alleviate symptoms but it doesn't usually treat an underlying cause. In a similar way, antidepressants can help, even though a medical exam will not reveal a "chemical imbalance." At this time, there are no blood tests to verify that a chemical deficiency is the cause of depression.

Should you take medication? Most likely you already are. If you aren't, make an informed and wise decision.

Medication vs. no medication. It is unclear whether medication is any more helpful than counseling. (And it is unclear whether counseling is any better, overall, than talking with a wise friend.) Even in cases of severe depression, careful analysis of the evidence does not always demonstrate the superior effectiveness of medication over secular counseling.[1] You would expect *at least* similar results when you allow Scripture to guide you.

Side effects. Any medication can have side effects. Antidepressants are no different. Overall, their side effects are not severe, but some people have such difficult reactions that they stop taking the medication. Dry mouth and difficulties in sexual functioning are among the more common side effects.

Long-term use. Although people have taken antidepressants for many years, we still aren't certain about their long-term effects. We know that some antidepressants lose their effectiveness over time – the so-called "poop out" effect. Also, there is increasing evidence that antidepressants are mildly addictive in the sense that you have to withdraw from them carefully. The problem with this process is that it is difficult to distinguish between the consequences of cutting back on medication and the depression itself. As a result, when you stop medication, you might mistakenly think your feelings of depression are returning when you are actually experiencing withdrawal symptoms.

Other cautions. Some have found that medication gives them the energy and clarity to work on depression-related issues in their lives. Others forget about the heart issues depression reveals because they have found relief and that is what they were after. The bottom line is this: don't put your hope in medication. Be thankful if it helps, but if it becomes just another place to put your hope instead of Jesus, you are just perpetuating the cycle of hopelessness.

Guidelines. If you are already taking medication, are you feeling better or worse than you felt before you started? If you are no different or worse, talk with your physician to discuss a

---

[1] Robert J. DeRubeis, Lois A. Gelfand, Tony Z. Tang, and Anne D. Simons, "Medications Versus Cognitive Behavior Therapy for Severely Depressed Outpatients: Mega-Analysis of Four Randomized Comparisons," *American Journal of Psychiatry,* 156 (1999), pp. 1007-1013.

change. Otherwise, become an expert on what God says to those who suffer and be quick to say, "Lord, search me."

If you are depressed and not taking medication, you could try medication immediately. But, if possible, delay that decision. Once you start medication, you tend to stay locked in to it.[2] Consider instead using some time to actively "take your soul to task" and relearn the gospel. Many people also suggest that regular exercise is helpful. These may alleviate your pain more than you expect. Another benefit of postponing medication is that it is easier to figure out what is helping if you introduce one "treatment" at a time. For example, if you started medication at the same time you started seriously considering your own heart, you wouldn't know if any improvements you experienced were from spiritual changes or medication.

Some depressed people are highly suicidal or passive in the extreme. These men and women, without doubt, are struggling with essential heart issues and you should persist in offering creative expressions of the gospel. Usually in such situations, however, families also pursue medical treatments in an effort to try anything reasonable to help. The main concern is if the depressed person has considered overdose as a suicidal plan. Since antidepressants can be lethal in large quantities, families should restrict the amount accessible to the depressed person.

When in doubt, get counsel from other pastors, counselors, physicians, or lay people who have biblical wisdom and experience with depression.

A Medical Exam

Easily overlooked in the discussion about medication is the

---

[2] S. A. Bull et al. "Discontinuation of use and switching of antidepressant drug treatment in depressive disorders: a systematic review," *Lancet,* 361 (2003), pp. 653-61.

fact that depression can be caused by a number of medical problems. In most cases, no treatable medical diagnosis can be found, but if your experience of depression is not clearly tied to particular circumstances, then consult a physician for a medical exam (Table 21.1).[3]

Table 21.1.
Medical Problems with Known Depressing Effects.

Parkinson's disease	Hyperthyroidism
Strokes	Hypothyroidism
Multiple Sclerosis	Cushing's disease
Epilepsy	Premenstrual depression
Head trauma	Viral or bacterial infections
Lupus (SLE)	Certain types of headaches
Vitamin deficiencies	Heart disease
Post-surgical changes	Side effects of medication
AIDS	Chronic Fatigue
Hepatitis	Any chronic illness
Post-partum changes	

In this list of medical problems, post-partum depression is one of the most recognizable. In minor and temporary forms, it is very common. Many women experience the blues after delivery because they have just experienced a physical upheaval and the body needs time to adjust. People who go through major surgery experience the same thing. Some women, however, experience depression that is more severe and long-

---

[3] Depressions from known diseases tend to feel different from those described in Chapter 2. The hopelessness, suicidal thinking, or self-loathing is missing.

lasting. The causes are unclear. Antidepressant medication might help, and women should be open to considering it. Also, since secular non-medical help, encouragement, and direction have been helpful for these women,[4] you would expect biblical help, encouragement and direction to be even more helpful.

Other Physical Treatments

Since depression is so common, and since there are no definitive medical cures, possible treatments have proliferated. Some of the more common include sun-mimicking lights (for those with a seasonal rhythm to their depression); St. John's Wort and herbal treatments; exercise; diet; megavitamins; and drugs not originally developed to treat depression, such as Mifepristone (a.k.a., RU-486, the abortion pill). More technical procedures include repeated transcranial magnetic stimulation and electroconvulsive therapy (ECT). ECT is of special interest because, after a time of decline in the 1970s and 1980s, it is once again a popular treatment for severe depression.[5]

The question with these physical treatments is not, "Is this treatment right or wrong?" The question is, "Is this treatment wise?" The guidelines of wisdom apply. For some treatments, such as moderate changes in diet and exercise, the risk and expense are minimal, so they do not demand extensive deliberation. But some of these treatments have higher risks. Therefore, wisdom calls for a careful investigation of the treatment, prayerfulness, seeking counsel from an experienced, wise group, and walking in the fear of the Lord.

---

[4] E.g., S. Stuart, M. W. O'Hara, & L. L. Gorman, "The Prevention and Treatment of Post-partum Depression," *Archives of Women's Mental Health*, 6 (Suppl.2), S57-S69.

[5] The UK ECT Review Group, "Efficacy and safety of electroconvulsive therapy in depressive disorders: A systematic review and meta-analysis," *Lancet*, 361 (2003), 799-808.

The Culture of Medical Treatments

We can be thankful that we live in an era when there are ways to alleviate the physical pain of depression. Still, it is worth examining the culture in which these treatments have emerged. For example, one feature of present-day thinking is that we still put our hope in medicine. Therefore, not only can medicine become idolatrous to us, but any treatment that comes with the veneer of medical science is likely to intensify a placebo effect. By that I mean that a medical treatment can change the experience of depression *not* because it is a successful treatment in itself, but because we have put our hope in that treatment, and our hope is what revises our experience of depression.

We also live in a culture that assumes we are only physical beings. Given that assumption, medication and other physical treatments are seen as the only possible ways to help. But we are also spiritual beings, and fundamentally so. We all live in the presence of God. When we recognize our spiritual core, we find that there are places in our lives that go deeper than any medication can reach.

Finally, our culture no longer sees any value in hardships. Although we all know that hardships have refined our character and matured us, we still try to escape suffering when it comes. This certainly isn't to say that we should pursue hardships or continue in pain when there are safe means to alleviate it, but hardships simply feel different when we know that God uses them to refine and change us.

With these issues in mind, be careful. Choose wisely.

Response

Discussions about medications and other physical treatments tend to provoke strong and sometimes extreme responses. It you have been hurt by medications, you oppose them. If you have been helped, you advertise them. Scripture, as is its custom, takes a third position that encourages wisdom, opens our eyes to larger issues in the culture, and keeps its focus on the heart.

CHAPTER 22

For Families and Friends

This chapter speaks first to the person who is depressed, then to family and friends.

If You Are Depressed

Depression can be hard on relationships. If you are depressed, you need relationships but you isolate yourself. You want help but you reject most counsel. You get encouraging words from others but you don't believe them. And if family or friends get frustrated, you say you predicted it all along. You act as though you were just waiting for them to get frustrated with you, perhaps even hoping for it. You believe you are worthless, and you seem bent on proving it.

One of the well-established findings about depression is that depressed people usually are not pleasant company.

> Depressed people enact a wide assortment of inappropriate verbal and nonverbal social behaviors that tend to elicit hostility and rejection from others. Through their behavior, depressed individuals create

around themselves social worlds that virtually guarantee a steady supply of negative evaluations.[1]

How do you respond? It may not be relevant to you, but if you react against such an observation, consider your response.

Does it make you feel guilty? Then keep it simple. You *are* guilty if you have sinned against other people. If you have sinned, confess it to God and others; give thanks because of God's delight in you as you confess; and ask for power to change.

Does it make you feel hopeless or helpless? Do you feel like other people simply don't understand depression? Consider this: nothing can keep us from loving other people – not the sins of others, not our infirmities, not our humanity. Certainly, such a task might seem impossible – and it is, if you ignore the cross of Jesus. But when we call out for the grace to love others more deeply, God always answers "Yes."

Resist depression on this point. Don't let it excuse you from relationships and love; you will just deepen your despair. Loving others is not simply a duty; it is the way you are designed. God created you to trust him and love others. When you are not trusting or not loving, you are disconnected from your purpose, and hopelessness will thrive.

Plan to love. It will look different when you are severely depressed, but as long as you are still conscious, you can find grace from God to love others in ways like these:

- Thank them
- Greet them

---

[1] R.B. Giesler and W.B .Swann, Jr, "Striving to Confirmation: The role of self-verification in depression," in Thomas Joiner and James C. Coyne (eds.), *The Interactional Nature of Depression* (Washington, D.C.: The American Psychiatric Association, 1999), pp. 189-218.

- Pray for them
- Listen to them
- Touch them

If you stumble here, ask forgiveness of God and others. Ask others to pray that you would be able to love in a way that is noticeable, and set out to love again. If you are not even taking a step toward loving, your heart is being revealed.

You are venturing into new ground with this. You are going to do something when you don't feel like doing it. It isn't that you don't want to love; it is that you don't feel. Some buy the lie that such behavior is hypocritical. Why would you do something when your heart isn't in it? The truth is that it is heroic. It may be the first time in your life that you did something simply because of Jesus.

If You Are Family or Friend

Family and friends, you will also be stretched in the way you love. You may discover that your love has been accompanied by mixed motives. Perhaps you wanted to change the other person or make life easier for yourself more than you wanted to love because Christ has loved you. Like your depressed friend, you too will have to consider your motives and ask for prayer to love deeply from the heart.

Sometimes you will grow weary in loving. We all do. You will genuinely love, but it will seem fruitless or irrelevant. It won't seem to matter to the depressed person. But know this: your love makes a difference. That doesn't mean that one concerted push to love will snap anyone out of depression. By itself, your love will not change anyone.

No amount of love from other people – and there

was a lot – could help. No advantage of a caring family and fabulous job was enough to overcome the pain and hopelessness I felt.[2]

But depressed people, like all of us, are aware of kindness and love that is willing to sacrifice. Love always leaves its mark. As a result, depressed people who do best are cushioned by persevering love.

Your Discouragement

It is probably the passivity that will discourage you the most. Perhaps the most obvious challenge posed by depressed people is their apparent lack of passion or enthusiasm for anything. For close friends and family, this is difficult because our passions are what make us recognizable and unique to those around us. A passionless person seems different to other people. Not only does he seem unmovable, he just seems different. "He isn't himself." "I don't feel like I know the person I married anymore."

There are a few ways to prepare to love someone when the relationship no longer seems reciprocal. Foremost is to realize that you can no longer rely on natural affection. In the past, there was a give and take to your relationship with the depressed person. You enjoyed the person, and he or she enjoyed you. This dynamic interaction spawned a growing, caring relationship. Now, however, the relationship appears unilateral, which, of course, is not what we think of as a relationship. Very few people are willing to commit long term to such a one-sided arrangement. After an initial sprint of love, they give up.

This puts you in a position similar to that of your depressed

---

[2] K.R. Jamison, *Night Falls Fast: Understanding Suicide* (New York: Knopf, 1999), p. 291.

loved ones. They, too, can no longer rely on natural affection. The problem is *not* that they dislike you; it is more that they simply don't feel, or what they feel is different levels of pain, and relentless pain expels all other passions.

Without your normal relational passions to energize you, you have a tremendous opportunity. You too have the privilege of really loving as an expression of your trust in Jesus Christ and your love for him. This is one of the key spiritual skills needed by those who are depressed, and, typical of God's ways, it is exactly what you need as well.

The course you must travel is identical to the one we have just described for your friend. For example, can you quickly identify your purpose? Anything that falls short of "to know Christ and to love others for his glory, not my own" will leave you hopeless and powerless to love. One of the many unique features of God's ways is that we all shift back and forth between our roles as physician and patient. You need help and others need your help. You may never have struggled with depression yourself, but the issues surrounding depression are basic to all our lives.

What is your purpose?

Who is Jesus?

How can I grow in trusting him and expressing that trust in love to others?

This means that you can't rely on last year's knowledge as you come alongside someone who struggles with depression. When you talk about purpose, it must be personal. It must come from how you yourself found purpose. When you offer hope, it must be because you have found hope.

A professional counselor had tried everything to encourage a depressed counselee and nothing seemed to help. With nothing left to offer, she confessed her own impoverishment and then talked about what she personally had been learning from God's

Word. When she finished, she spent more time than usual praying for both herself and her counselee.

To the counselor's surprise, the counselee scheduled another appointment. As soon as the counselee entered the room again, she gave her assessment of the last meeting.

"That was the best time we ever had together. Why haven't you done that more often?"

The counselor had become another needy person rather than a dispenser of helpful information. She was no longer giving principles, she was giving testimony. The next step was obvious.

"God's ways are better than our own. Isn't it like him that when I would feel most needy and inadequate, I would say things that were most helpful? You're right; I should have done this all along. I also should have asked you to do it, because I want to learn from you. Next time we meet, why don't you share what you are learning or thinking about when you are reading Scripture?"

To help a depressed person, you don't need expert knowledge. You do need an awareness of your own spiritual neediness, a growing knowledge of Jesus, and an eagerness to learn from others, including the person you would like to help.

What Is Most Important

Without passion or keen spiritual clarity, those who are depressed find it nearly impossible to maintain a vision for the things that are most important. There is nothing emerging from their haze of despair to capture their attention. This, too, is recognizable to all of us because the world functions in a similar way.

Scripture anticipates this struggle. To counter it, God raises up ordinary people who remind us of the truth.

See to it, brothers, that none of you has a sinful, unbelieving heart that turns away from the living God. But encourage one another daily, as long as it is called Today, so that none of you may be hardened by sin's deceitfulness. (Heb. 3:12)

What depressed people need – what we all need – are daily reminders of spiritual reality. As the truth of Christ is impressed on our hearts, we must offer that to others, and they to us. The target is always Christ and him crucified. The words are not magic, but they are food for the soul. Don't get derailed. What you need is not something new. You simply need to persevere in applying old truths to present situations.

You don't have to apologize for reading Scripture to the depressed person, praying with her, or looking for the Spirit's work in everyday events. In the same way that perseverance is key for the depressed person, perseverance in "ordinary" ministry is key for you as well. The depressed person is loyal to his or her pessimistic interpretations; you must be loyal to a Christ-centered interpretation. If possible, offer Christ-centered interpretations in a way that is personal, meaningful (at least to you), and succinct, since depression can affect attention and concentration.

Work Together

Since you are more like a depressed person than different, think in terms of partnerships. You are working together to walk a difficult path. Sometimes you will be doing the heavy lifting (Gal. 6:2), but if you are walking together you will look for ways to share the load.

One mistake that families and friends can make in the early stages of depression is to make all the effort themselves. It is a noble sacrifice, but you can't walk that way for long. You can read to, pray for, exhort, and express love in many ways to depressed people, but you can't drag them to *your* goals. Your destination must be a shared goal.

The end goal is Christ. The near goals are sometimes infinitesimally small steps that bring structure to an existence that can feel aimless. Structure refers to boundaries, guidelines, accountability, reminders, and organized plans. The principle is this: the more painful and disabling the depression, the more important it is for counselors and friends to provide structure.

Structure could include the following:

He must be willing to be structured

- Go to bed and get up at the same times each day.
- Eat at appointed times.
- Exercise at appointed times.
- Have a schedule for the day.
- Write down one thing you agree to work on every day.
- Follow through on agreements you made with other people. Let your "yes" be "yes."

This structure is not simply imposed on an unwilling victim. It is a partnership among brothers and sisters in Christ. Also, it includes times of considering "why?" Remember and review God's purposes, and remind one another that the present training – though perhaps wearisome and hard – has eternal benefit (1 Tim. 4:8).

There are two ways to err when helping depressed people bring structure into their lives. One is to impose a pace that is beyond their ability, making them feel even more hopeless. Start slowly. Help people set very basic goals initially, and then work together to gradually increase the number of tasks and goals in a day.

The other way to err is to omit frequent times of accountability. At least daily accountability is best. Since this may continue for months, those who minister must develop a practical and wise pace for themselves, being willing to serve while also being mindful of their other responsibilities.

Interrupt as Needed

If your good friend suddenly insisted that you were an alien intent on murder, you would try to disabuse him of that inaccurate interpretation. You would try to understand why he developed such a perspective, but you would not sit idly by while you were being accused. Instead, you would seek to persuade the person of the truth. You might even rebuke the friend for his persistence in clinging to an interpretation despite all evidence and counsel to the contrary.

Likewise, when depressed people interject their skewed and self-defeating interpretations of life, you can't sit idly by. You need to challenge and interrupt their inaccurate interpretation because it is wrong and leads to deeper despair. This, of course, is normal behavior in loving relationships. With depression, however, friends sometimes don't pursue these normal interactions. Perhaps they are afraid that the depressed person will feel rejected. Perhaps they are afraid that the least provocation could lead to suicide. As a result, depressed people are often handled very gingerly. You feel as if you are carrying a torch around a bomb with a short fuse.

Wisdom and love, of course, must dominate your relationships with those who are depressed, as they should dominate any relationship. But if you find that you are increasingly reluctant to say important things, reconsider your path. Talk to someone who has been on a similar path. If you are slow to say the things you think are important, you are not really engaging in a relationship. As a rule, the closer the relationship, the more open you should be with the other person.

Don't hesitate to interrupt the flow of despair, self-pity, and complaints that only reinforce the person's unbiblical interpretations of God and himself. To do this too early in your relationship with depressed people (or anyone) communicates that you don't really want to understand. It can silence people. But when your purpose is explained, it can be easily understood as an expression of love.

> I'm going to stop you for a second. Can you hear what's happening? The more you talk, the more you despair. I can see it in you. In fact, I can feel it in myself. Here is a plan. From now on, when I see the wave of depressive and, actually, unbiblical interpretations of life crashing down on you, I am going to point it out and try to run from it with you.

Response

There is more to persevering than you thought. It is not simply a word that appears briefly in Scripture. It is a powerful, deeply spiritual response to struggles that don't quickly disappear. When we persevere with one another, we are imitating one of the glorious facets of the character of God.

It is here, in persevering with someone who struggles with depression, where you have the advantage over the experts. Experts consult; then move on. Friends and family keep at it.

Yes, depression can eat at the heart of a relationship, but you also might notice God's blessing as you persevere. "Looking back, I would say that sticking with the person you love through the stressful dramas of mood disorder can eventually be incredibly rewarding."[3]

The word "ordinary" has come up often. This is not to diminish in any way the beauty and power of Spirit-driven ministry, because God's work is always extraordinary. It is, however, to emphasize that God has determined that we will best encourage one another through means that don't demand technical expertise. Scripture's wisdom is public domain. If we start to say things that draw attention to our own insights and wisdom, we are probably missing the normal means God uses to change us.

---

[3] Rose Styron, "Strands" in Nell Casey, Ed, *Unholy Ghost: Writers on Depression* (New York: HarperCollins, 2002), p.137.

CHAPTER

23

What Has Helped

Each person is different. A story that clicked for one person might be incomprehensible to the next. A strategy that seemed essential for you might be meaningless for someone else. Therefore, the following lists of ideas are intended to prime the pump rather than serve as an endless to-do list. They are specific ideas that have helped other depressed people.

"I felt like things began to change when..."
The first list comes from people who were once depressed. They were asked to finish this sentence: "I felt like things began to change when ..."

1. I began to talk to myself rather than listen to myself. I began to speak different Scriptures to myself rather than listen to my own voices of hopelessness.

2. I stopped saying, "It doesn't work." I was always looking for *the* answer. I would pray (trying to

make deals with God), look at my own heart (for a minute of two), or briefly try some other seemingly spiritual activity. When they didn't work, I would quit. I felt justified in quitting. Now I believe that it does "work." There is contentment and even joy in long-term, small steps of faith and obedience.

3. I had a pastor who kept the bigger picture of God's kingdom in front of me. Depression made my world so small; when I saw that God was on the move, I began to have hope.

4. My daughter became very sick. It forced me to see outside my own world.

5. A friend didn't give up on me. She was always loving me and pointing me to the truth, even when I didn't want to hear about Jesus.

6. A friend let me "borrow" her faith. My faith was so weak, but I always knew that she was confident of God's presence and love, for the church and even for me.

7. I forgave my father.

8. I heard many stories of sorrow and victory from friends.

9. I saw that it was 90 percent pride. I felt like I deserved certain things from certain people. It had been about me.

10. A friend who knew me well told me I was being a martyr. It shocked me at first, but I knew she loved me, and I knew she was right.

11. I began to believe that I was in a battle and realized that I had to fight.

12. I saw that I was doing things rather than just

having things done to me. For example, I was *doing* anger; I was *doing* big time complaining. In my heart, I was doing what I wanted.

13. Medication.

14. A friend who helped me to move from the "tyranny of the should" to living out of the gospel of grace.

15. I realized that my interpretations were fallible. I had huge misunderstandings and made many false accusations.

16. I began to force myself to read Scripture and listen to it.

17. I began to understand God's grace. I began to see that my wallowing in guilt was a form of works righteousness, not godly sorrow.

18. Once I saw that it was good to see my sin, I began to tell myself, "When in doubt, repent."

19. I decided.

20. I don't really know what God used. It was lots of little things.

"It was not helpful when..."

This second list consists of things that *were not* helpful. "It was not helpful when..."

1. I looked for superficial sins in my life. I was focused on specific sins, like the way I spoke to my children. I didn't look for the sin that drove my deeper sense of need.

2. I was angry, and no one tried to understand what my anger said about my relationship with God. They just said I needed to do the right thing.

Chapter Twenty-three

3.   I was angry, and people told me I had a right to be angry.

4.   I was told to love myself more.

5.   I was told to lower my expectations for myself.

6.   People gave answers before they tried to listen. It seemed like everyone had a remedy for me.

7.   People talked too much.

8.   Friends didn't say some of the things on their minds. They were afraid to speak honestly because they thought I was too fragile to hear it.

9.   People tried too hard.

Specific Strategies to Try

The following list contains homework assignments and specific strategies that have been helpful for some people.

1.   Take one biblical story, read it every day, and write down ten (or more) applications of it. (The basic idea with this assignment, and some of the others that follow, is that you want depressed people to meditate on something. Otherwise, their minds will drift further into despondency. As a helper, you may be tempted to try everything you can think of rather than stick with one thing until the person does it. If a depressed person can see the merit in this battle strategy, and he or she is willing to do it, stay with the assignment until it is done.)

2.   Find ten positive qualities in a friend. Write them down and send the list to him.

3.   Write out your purpose for living. Allow it to be revised by others. Then memorize it.

4. Become an expert in what God says to those who suffer. Consider starting with Hebrews 10-12.

5. Write down things from the Sunday sermon that are good, important, and true.

6. Each day, speak or write something that edifies others.

7. Take one aspect of creation (e.g., grass, a shrub, a squirrel, a leaf) and consider it until you can say it is good.

8. Listen to God's Word. Use music that points you to Christ, or ask someone to read to you or teach you what he is learning. Be able to summarize what you heard. Practice listening.

9. Keep a sharp eye out for grumbling and complaining. Like gossip, these sins are acceptable in our culture, so we don't see their ugly roots. What does the grumbling or complaining really say?

10. Consider these questions: In this culture, have we forgotten the benefits of hardships? What are the possible benefits to suffering? (Ps. 119:67, 71; 2 Cor. 1:8-10; Heb. 5:8; James 1:3)

11. Since the label "depression" cannot capture the complexity of your experience, what other words (especially words that can be keyed to Scripture) more concretely capture what is going on in your heart?

12. Get help. Ask a few people to pray for you and speak the truth to you. When you ask for prayer, ask for more than just the alleviation of depression. Use this as an opportunity to pray big prayers. Find some of the prayers in

Scripture and pray them. For example, pray that you would know the love of Christ (Eph. 3); pray that you would look more like Jesus (Rom. 8:29); pray that you would love others; pray that you would discern what it means today to bring glory to God.

13. You can't always change the way you feel, but you can change the way you think. What thoughts have to change? Start saying an emphatic "STOP" whenever you notice them.

14. Ask, *What am I getting out of my depression?* You might not have any answers, and the question might not be relevant, but it is a reminder that we are often doing more than we realize.

15. Write up a depression flow-chart. Begin with a recent event that sent you into a tailspin. Be as specific as possible about the steps you followed to restore your equilibrium.

16. What options do you have? You may feel like you are stuck on one long, hopeless path, but that isn't true. You are making decisions every day. Right now you are at another crossroads.

17. Search for a depressed person. Speak a word of encouragement.

18. Never go to Scripture without finding Jesus in it.

19. Be careful about analyzing on your own. Run your analysis by someone else.

20. Walk as briskly as you can with another person.

Now, with the pump primed, what would you add to these lists?

CHAPTER 24

What to Expect

Depression waxes and wanes. It can be ferocious for a short time and then recede into the background. It can be persistent for longer periods and then lose its grip, never to return. When it loses its intensity, the possibility that it is lying in wait can strike fear in the hearts of those who have been through it.

Like other human suffering, depression is difficult to predict. But even with its tendency to show up unannounced, there are still certain things you can expect.

Expect to be Forewarned

One reason to listen to depression is that you will realize that it has a history. It usually emerges for a reason. If you think of your own history of depression, you can find early warnings. For example, physical warnings could include fatigue and sleep changes. You lost interest in food. Colors were not quite as vibrant, and you didn't feel your usual responses to people and activities you once enjoyed. Spiritually, you might notice anger, loneliness, or a lack of comfort in remembering that the sovereign, loving God is in control.

Etch this in stone: if depression gives you an early warning – and it usually does – bring everything you have to the fight. Take your soul to task. Ask for help. Force-feed yourself Scripture and words of hope. Be on guard against self-pity, grumbling, and complaining. And keep the cross close at hand. If you let depression run its course, you will soon lose your vitality; you'll surrender. But with practice, you will notice that you have more resources than you thought to ward off the worst of the depression.

Expect to Be Taught about God and Yourself

A forty-year-old man who was prone to depressive swings wondered, as he noticed his deepening depression, "What will God teach me this time?" He was actually looking forward to what he would learn in God's schoolroom.

If you are willing to be trained by it, expect depression to be a good teacher. That doesn't mean that you should seek it out, and it certainly doesn't mean that you shouldn't try to alleviate it. But most people who are willing to be taught by suffering look back and are grateful.

Those with chronic illnesses can testify.

> Health is the best thing in the world except sickness. Indeed, knowing what God has done for me through physical weakness, and being persuaded that certain blessings could never have been given in any other way than through such an experience, I feel that it would have been nothing short of calamity to have missed the physical suffering through which I have passed.[1]

---

[1] H. W. Frost, *Miraculous Healing* (New York: R. Smith, 1931), pp. 45-46.

After three years in a Japanese prisoner of war camp, a British officer who found Christ in that camp said something that only a follower of Christ could say.

> "Well," he said, "it's all over. I wouldn't have missed it for anything. True, it was rough. But I have learned an awful lot that I couldn't have learned at university or anywhere else. For one, I've learned about the things of life that are real; and for another, I've learned that it is great to be alive." . . . Suffering no longer locked us up in the prison house of self-pity, but brought us into what Albert Schweitzer called the "fellowship of those who wear the mark of pain." We looked at the cross and took strength from the knowledge that it gave us, the knowledge that God was in our midst.[2]

Although these perspectives sound extreme, you find similar testimonies in every church. The benefits of hardship are well known. One of the arguments that counselors make against drug abuse is that it medicates away suffering so addicts avoid it rather than face it, walk through it, and learn from it. As a result, they can seem immature and short on character.

After Jesus, however, perspectives on suffering become even more radical. Now, suffering is viewed as the pains of childbirth rather than a purposeless, random, meaningless event. Since Jesus came, suffering is redemptive. It is part of the pilgrim's path, and it is a good one.

We also rejoice in our sufferings, because we know

---

[2] Ernest Gordon, *Miracle on the River Kwai* (Wheaton, Ill.: Tyndale, 1984), pp.158, 287.

that suffering produces perseverance; perseverance, character; and character, hope. (Rom. 5:3)

Suffering is a teacher. It taught Jesus (Heb. 5:8), and it can teach us. But it only truly teaches us as we fix our eyes on Jesus. If you avoid him in the midst of pain, expect to be embittered by it. But if you look to Jesus, you will no longer be alone. You will be strengthened and you will be changed. Expect to say, "This is exactly what I needed. Through depression I have learned things about God and myself. It would have been nothing short of a tragedy not to have learned them."

Expect God to Use You as You Love Others

One of the lessons God gives is about love. "And this is his command: to believe in the name of his Son, Jesus Christ, and to love one another as he commanded us" (1 John 3:23). Love God and love others – that is a summary of your purpose. If you are willing, expect to grow in loving others.

When we set out to love others even during our own suffering, the glory of Christ is unmistakable. It is just too unnatural to escape notice. When we are in pain, we usually aren't thinking about other people. We are only thinking about where to find relief. Yet the Spirit makes us look more like Jesus, and Jesus certainly loved others deeply even during intense pain and rejection.

But expect hindrances. On this side of heaven, love will not grow without a fight. Any time the glory of Christ is in reach, you will find a resistance in your own heart that is abetted by dark powers. Such warfare is found in a number of common responses.

"I tried that and it doesn't work."

"What's the point?"

"Jesus can do that, but I am not Jesus."

Or people just ignore it. The call to love doesn't even merit a response.

You, too, have excuses. When you embark on a plan to imitate the sacrificial love of Jesus, expect your heart's resistance. It reminds you once again that to follow Christ means that you need the Spirit of Christ. Love for others comes from saying, "Jesus, I need you." It comes out of faith and trust.

When you accept the challenge of loving others, expect more of your heart to be revealed because you are likely to love with strings attached. For example, you will love others *if* that will relieve your depression. "OK, God, I did my part. Now you do yours." Or you will love others *so* you can be loved by others. If love proceeds from anything other than "we love because he first loved us," expect to be disappointed.

If you are going to find joy in loving others, it will come from seeing that you have done something more important than relieving your depression. You have just seen the Spirit of God at work in your life. You have just seen evidence that you belong to Christ, and he is using you to accomplish his purposes.

Although the command to love others is simple, it is very unnatural to love, especially when we feel so empty. Expect the unnatural in your life. Expect that you are going to be an ambassador for the King of love.

Expect Depression to Feel "Light and Momentary"

The apostle Paul's most personal letter was his second letter to the Corinthians. Most of Paul's letters addressed the nature of the gospel. They were not highly autobiographical. But in Corinth, he was under attack. False teachers were suggesting that Paul was not qualified to speak with authority. In this context, he spoke very personally.

What he highlights in particular, as a way to establish his apostolic credentials, is that he has suffered great pain and hardship because of the gospel of Christ.

- His hardships were so severe that he assumed he was going to die (1:8), again and again (11:23).
- He was "hard pressed on every side," "perplexed," "persecuted," and "struck down" (4:8-9).
- He was beaten with rods threes times, flogged with forty lashes five times (11:24-25), imprisoned, and the focal point of a riot (6:5).
- He was stoned and left for dead (11:25).
- He often went without food and sleep (6:5).
- He was shipwrecked three times and once spent the night on the open sea (11:25).
- He lived with a disabling malady (12:7).

The point is this: when Paul speaks about suffering, he has credibility. Some people say that, yes, Jesus suffered, but he was God, so he could handle it. This, of course, is a purposeful maneuver to keep Jesus at a distance and justify self-pity. But it is impossible to try this excuse with Paul. Paul was a person like us, and his sufferings were more intense than our own.

With this in mind, consider his assessment of his life.

We do not lose heart. Though outwardly we are wasting away, yet inwardly we are being renewed day by day. For our light and momentary troubles are achieving for us an eternal glory that far outweighs them all. So we fix our eyes not on what is seen, but on what is unseen. For what is seen is temporary, but what is unseen is eternal. (2 Cor. 4:16-18)

He pronounces his suffering "light and momentary" and he is still suffering!

Envision a scale – an old-fashioned scale where a known weight was put on one side and the items to be weighed were placed on the other. If the original weights were honest, you knew how much your items weighed when the scale balanced.

Paul is saying that, indeed, suffering is very weighty and oppressive. But what he has received in Jesus Christ is even weightier. It more than counterbalances the scales of suffering, making it seem light and ephemeral in comparison.

It sounds impossible, or at least exaggerated, but we all have experienced something similar. A child falls and scrapes her knees, but her cries stop as soon as she is given a lollipop. The pain has not disappeared, but the joy of a lollipop outweighs it. Even better, a child scrapes her knees, but her cries stop as soon as she is embraced by her mother. The pain has not disappeared, but the child has something even better.

A woman loses her job due to downsizing, only to be hired five minutes later by the firm in the next office – at a higher rate of pay. We are all familiar with bad things that are outweighed by something much better.

For Paul to counterbalance the weight of his sufferings, he needed something extraordinary, and he found that in Jesus. This alone should be hopeful to you. It is like meeting a person who has gone through severe depression and says, "I made it. I am much better. You can be too." Even without knowing how this person made it, you are encouraged that it is possible.

Paul is happy to share his remedy with you, and he makes it clear that it is available to anyone who wants it, no matter who you are — however old, sick, or hurt.

Do you think God is stingy? Yes, you do. But Paul reminds you that he has made scads of promises and they are all "yes" (2 Cor. 1:20). Will he forgive? Yes. Will he never leave? Yes. Will he love with an everlasting love? Yes. Will he show unlimited patience? Yes. Will he make you his bride? Yes.

Do you know what you look like when you seek Jesus? Think of Moses when he came down from the mountain. He was a blaze of glory. His face shone with the reflected light of God in such a way that he had to wear a veil until the glory faded. Paul alluded to that story when he said that "we, who with unveiled faces all reflect the Lord's glory, are being transformed into his likeness with ever-increasing glory, which comes from the Lord, who is the Spirit" (2 Cor. 3:18). These are some of the reasons why Paul's suffering seemed light and momentary. In light of what he had received, his pain was minimal in contrast.

But it wasn't only what he had received. It was also what he was *going* to receive. Paul delighted in the present benefits of the cross, but he knew enough about misery and sin that his sights were always set in front of him. He was especially looking forward to the eternal glory — the glory that was to come. Somehow, that hope changed everything.

Response

Depression gives you tunnel vision. Scripture gives you vistas that extend from the beginning of creation to eternity. If you aren't dazzled by the expanse that Scripture lays in front of you, be persistent. As you keep looking, you will see more and more. One of your goals is to let the apostle Paul be your eyes until you can see more clearly.

PART FOUR   *Hope and Joy: Thinking God's Thoughts*

CHAPTER 25

Humility and Hope

In a story, the ending makes all the difference. A tragic story like Shakespeare's *Romeo and Juliet* starts well, with people full of hope and love, but it ends badly. A comedy like *Much Ado About Nothing* opens with dark omens and scheming betrayers. The future looks very uncertain but it turns out wonderfully. It is the ending rather than the humor that makes it a comedy.

You must decide whether you will live life as a tragedy or a comedy. The story that Jesus offers you is a comedy.

When you are watching a good comic movie for the first time, you are tense and on the edge of your seat because you don't know where the story is going. You want the best for the main characters, but something always seems to interfere. When you finally reach the end, and the heroes live happily ever after while the villains get their due, you relax. Shakespeare was right – *All's Well That Ends Well*.

Now watch the play or movie a second time. This time you are familiar with the plot. The difficulties are still there, and it looks like everything is headed for ruin, but you are hopeful.

You are alert to the signs that things will soon go well. There isn't the fear or heaviness that accompanied the first viewing. You still go through a range of emotions. You cry and laugh at the same points. But you interpret the entire story by its climax. Like a reader who reads the last chapter first, you see the hardships in a very different light.

Scripture tells you the end, and, if you have put your faith in Jesus rather than in yourself, it is your end too. Jesus wins. His justice prevails. His love is seen for what it really is – boundless and irresistible. Our unity with him exceeds our imaginations. We will see that life was much more purposeful than we thought. Everything we ever did by faith – because of Jesus – stands firm and results in "praise, glory and honor when Jesus Christ is revealed" (1 Peter 1:7). Knowing this, of course, does not blot out sorrow. As Nicholas Wolterstorff writes in *Lament for a Son*, we are "aching visionaries."[1] But knowing the end reveals that sorrow and death don't win. For those who know Christ, life and joy are the last word.

God's Story

By now you understand that hope is a key issue in depression. The critical transition is from hopeless to hopeful. You also understand that God makes promises, and he is pleased when we anticipate their fulfillment. God prizes hope. It says to him that we will not try to find our homes on earth, but we will look forward to the very best – to find our home in his presence.

> One thing I ask of the LORD, this is what I seek: that
> I may dwell in the house of the LORD all the days of

---

[1] Nicholas Wolterstorff, *Lament for a Son* (Grand Rapids: Eerdmans, 1987), p.86.

my life, to gaze upon the beauty of the LORD and to seek him in his temple. (Ps. 27:4)

Hopelessness means that

- you are unwilling to wait
- you want something more than you want Jesus
- you don't really know Jesus.

While our culture elevates riches and health, hope is one of the most coveted spiritual possessions. You get it by asking for it and by practicing it. You practice it by remembering and meditating on God's story.

Without God's story, everyone should be depressed, hopeless, and despairing because, with all the counterfeit stories, everything we deeply cherish comes to ruins in the end. There simply is no hope. "Why bother?" colors everything. Apart from the story of the cross and the resurrection, we are people who just sold our house to a developer. Settlement is tomorrow and the plan is to raze the house and use the property as a parking lot. In such a case, you would *not* buy new carpets, prune the shrubs, or paint the eaves. The property will be destroyed anyway; why invest so much effort and money?

Even the story of science, with all its confidence that we can make things better, ultimately can't give hope. A Nobel laureate might make impressive discoveries, but he knows that his work only scratches the surface, will be read by few, will be surpassed by others, and will do nothing to conquer death.

"The more the universe seems comprehensible, the more it seems pointless . . . . The effort to understand the universe is one of the very few things that lifts human life a little above the level of farce, and gives it some of the grace of tragedy."[2]

The "grace of tragedy." Apart from the telling of a different story, that is the most we can hope for. Perhaps "the grace of tragedy" is enough for those who find a certain romance and heroism in a completely pessimistic and lifeless endpoint, but such a perspective is a luxury reserved for those who have somehow found temporary hope within themselves. For the rest of us, "modernity was defined by the attempt to live in a universal story without a universal storyteller."[3] In post-modernity, there is neither universal story nor storyteller.

God's story goes from eternity to eternity. It starts with, "In the beginning, God." He is the Creator and we are his creatures. Immediately this retelling subverts all other stories. Other stories are always looking for ways to humanize God and deify us, but God's story exalts him and brings appropriate humility to us as his creatures. All wisdom starts here. If you miss it, you are on the wrong path and without hope.

Words of comfort often begin with God reaffirming that he is the Creator and we are his creatures.

> "This is what the LORD says – your Redeemer, who formed you in the womb: I am the LORD, who has made all things, who alone stretched out the heavens, who spread out the earth by myself." (Isa. 44:24)

In this case, God's self-revelation as Creator is a comfort

---

[2] Jerry L. Walls, *Heaven: The Logic of Eternal Joy* (New York: Oxford, 2002), p.175.

[3] Walls, *Heaven*, p.174.

because it reminds us that there is no other god who can thwart God's intent. His plans will prosper. Also, it reminds those listening that they are not God. They are God's offspring, who owe allegiance to him and no other.

The story continues. He creates a people for himself but his people choose a different story. Yet God continues with his plan and pursues wayward creatures. There is hope throughout, but sin and death are prominent. That is why the authentic story of hope hinges on the resurrection of Jesus. It is God's answer to a hopeless world.

The resurrection of Jesus introduces the extended climax of God's story. It goes from the resurrection to his final return, when he announces the consummation of all things. During this climax, God assures us that those who have placed their faith in Jesus will also be resurrected, but final bodily resurrection will have to wait for Jesus' return. Jesus is the first-fruits, the elder brother who prepares the way. Our own final resurrection is stored in trust for us, so for now we wait. We wait with the expectation of someone who will soon give birth or soon be married, but we wait. And while we wait, we groan. Yet in the midst of our groaning, we hope. We live like Jesus who, in the midst of suffering, anticipated his resurrected life with the Father. If Jesus' life was rooted in hope, then we are honored and humbled that our lives can do the same.

Our Revisions to God's Story

If you are hopeless, there may be many contributors, but two are certain. First, you have placed your hope in something other than God – a person, money, personal reputation – and it has let you down. Second, you may understand that Jesus conquered death, but you live as though he is still in the grave. All hopelessness is ultimately a denial of the resurrection. It falsely prophesies that the last words are death, despair, meaninglessness, ruin, and nothing. Yet the resurrection trumps death, sin, misery and everything touched by the curse. Resurrection is the last word; as a result, "your labor in the Lord is not in vain" (1 Cor. 15:58).

Have you cried out to the Lord in your hardship? The resurrection says that such an act of faith has eternal value.

Have you sought to love in your hardship? The resurrection says that such an act has eternal value.

Have you sought to be humbly obedient to Jesus? Have you done anything because of Jesus? The resurrection says that this comes out of faith that will prove to be worth more than gold (1 Peter 1:7).

Some hopeless people who anticipate only death cite Scripture that says "I desire to depart and be with Christ" (Phil. 1:23). But Christ is not what hopeless people really want. The God-talk is misleading. The goal of hopelessness is to end the suffering, and if God happens to be there when it happens, fine. But God's presence is not essential.

Consider your own story. If you believe that Jesus is the risen Lord, then your story is this:

> I am created by God. I am his offspring; he is my Father. I have sinned, but like the father of the prodigal son, my Father has pursued me. He sent Jesus to be the sacrifice for my sin and redeem me from the grave and the Evil One. Now I live for the One who died for me but is alive. I fight against sin through the power of God's Spirit, and I look forward to the day when sin and suffering are over and I see Jesus face to face.

Notice the apostle Paul's rendering of the story. He begins with his resumé: he was circumcised, from the right Hebrew tribe, from the right guardians of the law, and he kept the law faultlessly.

> But whatever was to my profit I now consider loss for the sake of Christ. What is more, I consider everything a loss compared to the surpassing greatness of knowing Christ Jesus my Lord, for whose sake I have lost all things. I consider them rubbish, that I may gain Christ and be found in him, not having a righteousness of my own that comes from the law, but that which is through faith in Christ . . . . I want to know Christ and the power of his resurrection and the fellowship of sharing in his sufferings, becoming like him in his death, and so, somehow, to attain to the resurrection from the dead. (Phil. 3:7-11)

He could also tell a shorter story. "For to me, to live is Christ and to die is gain" (Phil. 1:21). Such a story makes hopelessness impossible.

What is your story? Your goal is to accept Scripture's telling of it and make it your own, but too often we add personal edits and devise alternate endings. We insert chapters about how we need something from this world, such as love from other people or personal success. We reason that we are only human, not recognizing that we were made for something much greater than putting our hopes in created things. We interject themes that run independent of our relationship with God. For example, one part of our story could be about what God has done, but another part is about our quest for independence. We leave the

Father's house and embark on our own journeys, and we foolishly hope in this life rather than in Jesus. We make our story about pain, and we climax it with the release of pain rather than with Jesus. All these emendations to God's story are guaranteed to result in hopelessness.

Better than Freedom from Pain

Most people believe that eternity will be better than the present. This, of course, is true for those who hope for Jesus' return. When we see Jesus, "there will be no more death or mourning or crying or pain" (Rev. 21:4). But there is something that is arguably even better. Therefore, if you are going to look forward to the gifts God gives us when we see him face to face, hope for this: when we see Jesus, *we will no longer be people who sin* (1 John 3:3).

Yes, that is what is better. Think of it. We will love God perfectly. We will love others without reservation. We will think less often of ourselves and delight in the fact that eternity is about God and not us. We will be thrilled by the fact that God's glory is on display for all his people to see; being pain-free will be no more than a pleasant realization that occasionally sneaks into our awareness. Given a choice, a sinless eternity with the loving God is much preferred over a pain-free one where sin still bedevils.

Be certain to incorporate this into your story. You are becoming what you were intended to be – a sinless child of the Most High God.

Hope on This Side of Heaven

When you purposefully make God's universal story your own, you will always be looking in two directions. You will be looking backward to the cross and looking forward to the time when you see Jesus, the object of your hope.

When we look back at the cross we see forgiveness of sin, the love and generosity of God to sinners, the fact that we now approach God without fear, the righteousness we receive rather than earn. These and many other promises are "yes," and they radically change the present. We can live as people who have been given a great gift, so there is a persistence of thankfulness and joy. We have no reason to think we must repay God for our sins. We have no reason to fear. We don't have to play it safe.

> Living means choosing, and choosing means running
> the risk of making mistakes, and accepting the risk of
> being guilty of making mistakes.[4]

The cross means that we have freedom to make mistakes.

The resurrection of Jesus confirms that he truly was the Son of God with power; it redirects our attention to the future resurrection of all who believe. It points to heaven, and heaven is what brings meaning to the present. It means that your house will not be sold to a developer. Someday it will be a thing of great beauty, so you *do* change the carpets, work the garden, and paint the exterior. You know that your work will not be in vain; the master builder has determined that your less-than-professional attempts will contribute to the final masterpiece. Nothing we do because of Christ will be in vain. This brings purpose and diligence to the present.

But there is something else that hope does in the here and now. It opens our eyes so that we, like the psalmist, can see the ongoing work of God. The psalmist says, "I am still confident

---

[4] Paul Tournier, *Guilt and Grace* (New York: Harper and Row, 1962), p. 107.

of this: I will see the goodness of the LORD in the land of the living" (Ps. 27:13). The truth of God's story is that he is on the move right now. He is changing us, enlarging his church, and bringing all history to a climax.

The book of Revelation is the best-known teaching that God is presently at work. It is written to people who are going through great suffering, wondering if evil actually wins so that the church gradually is brought to nothing. To encourage them, God parts the curtain of heaven so his people can see that the armies of God are on the move *now*. God both is winning and has won.

When you know that God's strategy is playing out perfectly, you see much more. For example, let's say that you are watching the Olympic 10,000 meter run. Your favorite runner seems to be struggling in the middle of the pack. You might be tempted to interpret every grimace as further evidence that she won't win, and with every lap you are more certain of eventual defeat. But what if you know more details, such as the fact that her best time is more than twenty seconds better than anyone else in the field? Or the fact that she usually stays with the pack until the last two laps and then suddenly accelerates to a pace that can't be matched? Or the fact that she *always* seems to be struggling – that is just the way she runs? If you know these things, you will interpret the race differently. You will be optimistic, confidently pointing out the strategy, and interpreting her grimace as a personal trademark rather than a cause for alarm.

When you look around at yourself and the world around you, it is easy to be pessimistic because the future doesn't always look very promising. But when you know the conclusion – that the church will win and Christ will reign – you are able to see the Spirit of God move in the details.

Ask God to open your eyes so you can see his goodness in the land of the living.

Humility

God's story is a great story. We, however, are people of habit. Change does not come easily or quickly. We stubbornly cling to past interpretations and old stories even when God's universal story is much better. The reason is not that we lack education and knowledge, but that we overflow with pride.

You have been crafting your own story for years. It isn't original, having been pieced together with scraps from your culture and people you admired, with your own unique twists. But it is your own. To adopt a different story, with a different hero, means that we must say, "I was wrong." Given the options, many of us opt to stay with our old story.

Deep change is rarely a matter of knowledge. It is a matter of repentance. We have chosen a path apart from God; repentance is the process of turning back. We have chosen a different story, filled with subtle lies about God, questioning his love, care and compassion. Repentance means to renounce our story and believe that there is only one Storyteller. God alone is authorized to interpret our lives.

Hope will only grow in the ground of humility.

Response

This is such a critical issue that it is worth an extended response.

First, note that there is an edge to hope. It refuses to surrender and sit passively while misery abounds. "Hope finds in Christ not only a consolation *in* suffering, but also the protest of the divine promise *against* suffering."[5] Hope says that things are not now the way they are supposed to be, and it actively partners with God to bring in the consummation of his

---

[5] Jurgen Moltmann, *Theology of Hope* (New York: Harper & Row, 1967), p. 21.

kingdom. It is an act of rebellion against the status quo.

Second, if hope is nothing more than believing the promises of God, the lack of hope is unbelief. Lack of hope reveals that we really don't believe what God has said. Therefore, it is sin.

Third, hope is a community affair. Church, like everything else for hopeless people, can seem irrelevant and meaningless. But one way it blesses us is that it reminds us of the true story. The songs, prayer, sermon and fellowship all serve to remind us of reality. When hopeless people attend church, they often come daring the preacher to say something that will be helpful to them. As a result, they miss the retelling of the story.

Hope is a skill that develops over time. It is also a corporate venture that needs the reminders of the body of Christ. Commit yourself to a church where the story is told, and seek opportunities for daily reminders.

And finally, here is a brief summary of this chapter: Learn to say "Come, Lord Jesus" (Rev. 22:20). This reminds you that your hope is in a person, and such a hope is certain. His response is, "Yes, I am coming soon" (Rev. 22:20).

What is your plan for growing in hope?

26
CHAPTER

Thankfulness and Joy

Every depressed person should set out to be an expert in joy. It is a no-risk proposition. The worst that can happen is that you will honor God (Ps. 126:1-2), be surprised that he promises you great gladness, and even taste something of joy in the midst of sorrow.

Truth be told, however, there *are* some barriers and risks that can make it difficult to pursue joy. Depression can sometimes be a familiar companion – a loathsome one but a companion all the same. Any time a difficult experience has some longevity in our lives, we can gradually derive some personal identity from it. For example, depression can be very powerful in the way it dominates relationships. For someone who has never really had an impact on others, depression changes things. It can make us the center of attention, the focus of people's concern.

Another risk is that depression usually wants something at the same time it fears getting it. What if the desire is satisfied, and there is still an underlying ache and despair? What then?

In frustration, we often think that what we would really like is to have all of our desires and emotions satisfied. . . . . But no understanding of the passions is possible until we come to appreciate this all-important and perhaps surprising feature: that their unsatisfied existence is, in general, often more important to us than their successful expression and satisfaction.[1]

If anger is in any way a piece of your depression, the possibility of joy creates a challenging predicament. When you think that others, including God, have wronged you, there is a difficult choice to make when they do something unusually kind. Consider a six-year-old girl who is angry because she had to do her chores before going out to play. To display her anger and indulge her self-pity, she does her chores very noisily, then shuns her parents and sequesters herself in her room. So far, so good. But what will she do when her parents invite her out for ice cream and miniature golf? If she says no, she hurts herself because she loves both ice cream and miniature golf. If she says yes, she has to humble herself and give up her snit, which would mean losing face. She decides to split the difference by going with her parents while doing her best to look miserable. Every time she makes a putt, she must mask her joy.

In other words, there is something marvelous about joy but there is something humbling in it too. Joy takes our attention off ourselves and places it on God and all the things that have God as their source – things that are true, noble, right, pure, and lovely (Phil. 4:8). You could split the difference and consider joy

---

[1] Robert C. Solomon, *The Passions: Emotions and the Meaning of Life* (Indianapolis: Hackett, 1993), p.160.

halfheartedly, but be forewarned: if you even crack the door open to joy, you will get more than you expected.

Joy and Thanksgiving Compared

We could just as easily have picked thankfulness as the area in which to develop expertise. Many Christian books you read on depression will push you – wisely – to practice thankfulness. The skill of thankfulness can hold the darkest depression at bay; it can even push back against depression and lighten it.

Thankfulness begins with a sense of our own desperateness. We are needy and unable to supply our own needs. Then comes someone who gives us what we couldn't give ourselves and our lot improves. We in turn are filled with gratitude and thanks.

When we come before God, thankfulness begins by knowing that we are spiritually destitute. We are sinners who can't help but sin and we deserve God's eternal rejection. God then pursues us, opens our eyes to his grace and mercy, and satisfies our deepest needs and spiritual thirsts. Our lot improves immensely. We in turn are forever thankful.

Most gifts are one-time events, but God's mercies are new every morning (Lam. 3:23) and his love is forever. Therefore, we always give thanks.

> Give thanks to the LORD, for he is good; his love
> endures forever. (Ps. 107:1; 118:29, 136)

You can't go wrong if you let Scripture give you reasons to be thankful. Keep a pad and paper next to your Bible to write down those reasons every time you read. You could also use your mealtimes as opportunities to give thanks.

Even so, joy is better. Thanksgiving is gratitude for a benefit we have received. Joy includes gratitude, but its true delight is in the beauty of God and the deep goodness in all the things that come from him. Joy draws attention outward with a non-possessive appreciation for something that is good.

For example, you are in a boat and about to die. The winds have whipped the waters into a maelstrom that will engulf you within minutes. Jesus speaks a word and the waters are still. No one, however, thanks him. They are all too amazed (Matt. 8:23-27). This amazement at Jesus' power is the beginning of joy. It is not primarily self-referential. It is more than satisfied to contemplate the majesty of the One who just spoke.

Another example: You are blind. Jesus is coming and you call out for mercy. When he stops, he asks what you want. You ask for sight. When he gives it to you, you don't simply thank him, you follow him. This, too, is the beginning of joy. Your attention is captured by the Giver more than the benefit received (Matt. 20:29-34).

Thanks and thanksgiving can be found dozens of times in Scripture. Joy, gladness, rejoice and enjoy can be found hundreds of times.

Joy in Suffering

Joy is not the opposite of suffering. If it were, a person practiced in joy could crowd out pain because one couldn't exist with the other. Instead, joy can actually be a companion to suffering. You can see this at Christian funerals. These are grievous events in the church because of the loss of someone beloved. But they are also some of the most joy-filled as worshippers contemplate the glories of heaven and remember that death is not the last word.

To simultaneously say that some things are bad and others are good seems like a precarious balance, but that is the nature of this time in history. The curse and sin persist; they are bad and we wait with hope for their eradication. But the original goodness of creation can still be detected, and the glories of the cross and everything it ushered in are evident through Jesus. These, of course, are great blessings that we enjoy and for which we praise God. We continue to suffer, but suffering cannot rob us of the eternal joy that has already begun.

Job spoke of his "joy in unrelenting pain – that I had not denied the words of the Holy One" (Job 6:10). He took joy in the fact that he had not denied God or questioned his faithfulness throughout his ordeal. He did not take *pride* in this; he found joy. He knew that God saw his faithfulness as a good thing and Job himself saw it was good as well.

Now splice this together with God's promise that he will never let us be tempted in a way that makes sin inevitable (1 Cor. 10:13). This means that God will give you grace to avoid sin during depression, especially the sin of charging God with wrongdoing (Job 1:22). You too can have joy in the midst of unrelenting pain.

This is the precedent for "consider it pure joy... when you face trials of many kinds" (James 1:3). The joy in this case is not a denial of pain. It is joy that something wonderful is taking place. The person in trials has the opportunity to observe faith being refined, perseverance developed, and maturity attained. These are a joy to behold, whether they are being nurtured in us or in others.

Boredom and Depression

Before trying to identify the things that provoke joy, consider how depression overlaps with boredom. Boredom has much in common with depression and is sometimes key to it. It could be described as depression without pain.

Boredom is "the declaration that nothing possesses sufficient interest to be worthy of attention."[2]   It says, "I dare you, try to excite me – I'll bet you can't." Everything is flat and in shades of blue and gray.

You can become bored in one of two ways.

First, you may have your eyes wide open to the ugliness of life while you are blind to the shafts of glory that can be found almost anywhere, especially now that God's Spirit has been given. When you see no glory, there is not much in this world that is worth your attention.

Second, boredom is a form of pride. The bored person is too cool to be moved by the ordinary or popular.

> Cultivated and sophisticated observers have been known to dismiss as "boring" people they encounter, meetings they attend, sentiments they hear or read. To do so attests to the fineness of their sensibilities.[3]

Joy is the antidote for boredom. It says, "Look, God's glory is all around."

Looking for Joy

To have joy, you must be willing to look for it. You must be willing to welcome joy rather than feel like you are betraying your depression by looking for it. (And it is true – looking for joy is a betrayal of depression.)

As with hope, there is humility in joy. We have to acknowledge that we were wrong. We were betting that there was no beauty – in God or anything else – but there is. So start with confession and repentance. Confess that you have disagreed with God when he has said that there is good.

---

[2] Patricia Spacks, *Boredom: A Literary History of a State of Mind* (Chicago: Univ. of Chicago, 1995), p. 229.

[3] Ibid., p.252.

Confess that you have not even considered how to glorify him by pursuing joy, even though you know it is an obvious way to surprise a bored and pessimistic generation.

Looking for Joy in Creation. The most common place to look for joy is in creation. Scripture doesn't emphasize this, but it does assume that there is goodness in creation that points to the good Creator.

Oceans, mountains and anything big are favorites. A good friend chose something small. He had cultivated a rose garden that yielded beautiful blossoms, but he was too busy to appreciate them. His self-imposed assignment one day was to enjoy a rose. After dinner he brought a chair out to the garden, seated himself in front of a flower, and got to work. His goal was to enjoy its variegated color, scent, and overall beauty. Even if he had been unsuccessful on this first attempt – though he did enjoy the rose – he was on the right path because he was committed to looking. If there had been no pleasure in the rose, he soon would have found it in even better things.

The caution here is to allow the rose to be a signpost. If our pleasure extends only to the rose itself, we risk idolatry. Ultimate joy is not there. Instead, the rose says, "It is not I. I am only a reminder. Look! Look! What do I remind you of?"[4] Creation, no matter how beautiful, says, "We are not thy God, seek above us . . . he made us."[5]

Creation might be surprised by the way it elicits joy because, no matter how attractive it can be, there are better signposts all around us. Scripture portrays creation as groaning until it too is released from corruption (Rom. 8:22). Scripture also reveals that creation is more accustomed to being caught up in the joy

---

[4] C. S. Lewis, *Surprised By Joy* (New York: Harcourt, Brace & World, 1955), p. 220.

[5] Augustine, *Confessions* (New York: Pocket, 1952), X. p.178.

of God (Isa. 44:32) than it is being enjoyed itself. It would probably be uncomfortable with all the attention it receives.

> Say among the nations, "The LORD reigns."
>   The world is firmly established, it cannot be moved;
>   he will judge the peoples with equity.
> Let the heavens rejoice, let the earth be glad;
>   let the sea resound, and all that is in it;
>   let the fields be jubilant, and everything in them.
> Then all the trees of the forest will sing for joy;
>   they will sing before the LORD, for he comes,
>   he comes to judge the earth. (Ps. 96:10-13)

If creation is glad in the goodness of God, and if unborn children leap in the womb when they hear the news of the Messiah (Luke 1:44), then joy is within our reach as well.

Finding Joy in the Lord. The real object of joy, of course, is God. He is what all earthly joys reflect. Throughout history people have found great joy because the Lord is present (Ps. 21:6). God is the joy and delight of his people (Ps. 43:4).

This was Jonathan Edwards's test of true religion. Do you find joy in God?

> Joy . . . consists in the sweet entertainment their minds have in the view or contemplation of the divine and holy beauty of these things [the character of God], as they are in themselves. And this is the main difference between the joy of the hypocrite and the joy of the true saint. The former rejoices in himself . . . the latter rejoices in God.[6]

Some find the thought of heaven boring. But once you start finding joy in the Lord, you will find an inexhaustible delight. Day after day you will find new divine beauty to enjoy, and the search will continue for all eternity.

Remember the summary of Scripture offered by the authors of the Westminster Shorter Catechism? "What is the chief end [aim] of man? To glorify God and enjoy him forever." The summary is truthful. God is the God of joy and gladness, he freely and liberally gives joy to his people, and he actually commands us to search for it in him (Ps. 106:4-5; 1 Thess. 5:18). Therefore, the psalmist truly understands God's thoughts when he prays, "Let me hear joy and gladness; let the bones you have crushed rejoice" (Ps. 51:8). This is not a selfish prayer; it is purposeful. The psalmist wants to be what he was intended to be, the person every follower of Christ will one day be – a joyful worshiper.

Noticing Joy in the True, Noble, Right, Pure and Lovely. Knowing that joy comes from God, we are freed to take joy in the things he has blessed. He is the God "who richly provides us with everything for our enjoyment" (1 Tim. 6:17). "Everything" good can produce quite a list.

Eating, drinking, working (Eccl. 5:18-20)
God's law ((Ps. 19:8)
Bearing his name (Jer. 15:16)
Love and unity that points others to the divine lover (John 15:11-12; 1 John 1:3-4)
Faith and obedience in others (2 Cor. 7:4; Phil. 1:25; 3 John 1)
A cheerful look (Prov. 15:30)

---

6 Jonathan Edwards, *Religious Affections* (New Haven: Yale Univ., 1959), p. 240.

Chapter Twenty-six

Justice (Prov. 11:10)
Wisdom in others (Prov. 10:1), and the ability to offer
wisdom and comfort to others (Prov. 15:23)
Comfort given to those you love (2 Cor. 7:7)
People knowing Christ (1 Thess. 2:19)
Receiving salvation (1 Peter 1:8)
Joy in others (2 Cor. 1:24)

The list can be endless: the laughter of children, the honoring
of the righteous, the perseverance of the depressed, persecuted,
or infirm, the pouring out of God's Spirit evident throughout
the world.

Notice that many objects of joy are other people and their
Christ-likeness. If God says that creation is good and we can
enjoy it, how much more can we enjoy people, the part of
creation that he proclaims "very good"? If God takes delight in
you and others, then you can as well.

The LORD your God is with you, he is mighty to
save. He will take great delight in you, he will quiet
you with his love, he will rejoice over you with
singing. (Zeph. 3:17)

Present-day life is complicated. There is misery now but
great hope for the future. God has already begun the renewal
that will take place, so there are opportunities for joy today, not
just when eternity arrives.

Our Double Joy

As you look for joy, you have access to a double pleasure.
You will find joy in Christ and what he has done, and you will
find joy in sharing God's joy.

A few years ago, my wife asked me to read one of her favorite books. When I finally read it, the book was a pleasure. I enjoyed its content and the way it was written. That, of course, happens any time we read a good book. But since I knew that this book had been a joy to my wife, my enjoyment had an added dimension. It brought a kind of unity that comes when people share the same delights. Not only did I enjoy knowing my wife's joys better, but I actually shared her joy.

My wife has interests that I don't share as passionately, and I am glad that she has them. I am blessed by them. But it is one thing to be happy for my wife when she experiences something especially joyful, and it is another to share in it. It creates a bond and a mutual understanding that are joys in themselves.

This is the double delight of joy. We enjoy what God has given us, and there is a bond – a knowing smile – that we share with him as we participate in his joy. True joy comes as when we learn to enjoy the things that God enjoys.

Response

Joy takes practice. Study joy in the Psalms. Psalmists didn't even know the details of Jesus' love but, with their glimpses of God's love, they had joy and gladness. If you are willing to look for joy, the psalmists can lead you to it. The goodness of God is shot through creation and the church, so joy is always possible. When you can't see it, return to the cross and appreciate the beauty of what Jesus did. Appreciate the beauty of his sacrifice – his willingness to become like us and give up everything. Appreciate the beauty of his love. Just behold it. Admire it.

Or consider Job's joy that he didn't deny his God in the midst of unrelenting pain. You could apply this by considering specific ways to love other people. Then take joy in the Spirit working within you.

God's splendor ascends over the sorrow of life. Joy is possible. Choose to become an expert in it. After all, joy is not something evanescent. What you will taste is "everlasting joy" (Isa. 35:10). It is here to stay, and the day is coming when those who know Jesus will be known by their joy. Believe it or not, you are becoming a joyous person. You *will be* a joyous person.

Some say that joy is the serious business of heaven. But don't think that this is just for the sweet by-and-by. The kingdom of heaven began with power when Jesus came, so you can get into the family business even now.

The Final Word

Jazz musicians have understated their musical art by saying, "There are only twelve notes you're messing with; just play them all and make sure you end on the right one." When faced with depression, Scripture's musical score includes many more than twelve notes. For sheer breadth and depth it is without equal. Its wisdom is layered and dense. But sometimes it can seem like too much, and every time you try to follow through on a biblical truth you get lost. *Mary Had a Little Lamb* suddenly becomes an atonal composition with no discernible direction. You have completely botched it. When this happens – and, to be sure, it will – just try to keep playing and end on the right note.

The Psalms are your model.

But I trust in your unfailing love. (Ps. 13:5)

I am still confident of this: I will see the goodness of the LORD in the land of the living. Wait for the LORD; be strong and take heart and wait for the LORD. (Ps. 27:13-14)

> The LORD's unfailing love surrounds the man who
> trusts in him. (Ps. 32:10)

When you read a letter from someone whose love is very important to you, your heart can rise and fall many times. In one paragraph you think you have found an expression of tenderness; in another it sounds like ordinary news or possible hints of dissatisfaction with you. Then you get to the final words.

"Warmly" is what a brother or sister would write. Many writers can casually end a letter with "Love." But the final words of this letter are, "I love you." They are unmistakable. Although you don't understand how or why, you are clearly the object of this person's affection. For the rest of the day you are changed by the memory of those final words. People notice a bounce in your step or hints of vitality that were missing the day before.

When you feel lost or confused, get to these final words. The fact that Jesus Christ came to earth to die in our place is his resounding "I love you." Since his love is dependent on himself rather than on you, you are not in danger of being unloved on those days when you feel utterly faithless. In fact, at those times his love will be even more surprising and precious, because you will remember that this extravagant love is undeserved and unearned.

Your own heart has much to say, but let Jesus have the final word.

"Grace" is the shorthand. In that one word, God takes us out of ourselves and turns our attention onto him, the One who showers forgiving love on us even when we don't realize all he has forgiven. It is brimming with promises and guarantees. No wonder the apostle Paul began almost every letter with "Grace and peace to you from God our Father and the Lord Jesus Christ" (Gal. 1:3). And it was his pleasure to end the same way: "May the grace of the Lord Jesus Christ, and the love of God, and the fellowship of the Holy Spirit be with you all" (2 Cor. 13:14).

In your battle with the manifold features of depression,

Grace to you.

Scripture Index

OTHER BOOKS BY OUR AUTHORS

Addictions – A Banquet in the Grave: Finding Hope in the Power of the Gospel. Edward T. Welch shows how addictions result from a worship disorder – idolatry – and how they are overcome by the power of the gospel. *0-87552-606-3*

Age of Opportunity: A Biblical Guide to Parenting Teens, 2d ed. Paul David Tripp uncovers the heart issues affecting parents' relationship with teenagers. *0-87552-605-5*

Blame It on the Brain? Distinguishing Chemical Imbalances, Brain Disorders, and Disobedience. Edward T. Welch compares the roles of the brain and the heart in problems such as alcoholism, depression, ADD, and homosexuality. *0-87552-602-0*

Instruments in the Redeemer's Hands: People in Need of Change Helping People in Need of Change. Paul David Tripp demonstrates how God uses his people, who need change themselves, as tools of change in the lives of other. 0-87552-607-1

Seeing with New Eyes: Counseling and the Human Condition through the Lens of Scripture. David Powlison embraces, probes, and unravels counseling and the problems of daily life with a biblical perspective. *0-87552-608-X*

Step by Step: Divine Guidance for Ordinary Christians. James C. Petty sifts through approaches to knowing God's will and illustrates how to make biblically wise decisions. *0-87552-603-9*

War of Words: Getting to the Heart of Your Communication Struggles. Paul David Tripp takes us beyond superficial solutions in the struggle to control our tongues. *0-87552-604-7*

When People Are Big and God Is Small: Overcoming Peer Pressure, Codependency, and the Fear of Man. Edward T. Welch exposes the spiritual dimensions of pride, defensiveness, people-pleasing, needing approval, "self-esteem," etc. *0-87552-600-4*

Booklet Series: *A.D.D; Anger; Angry at God?; Bad Memories; Depression; Domestic Abuse; Forgiveness; God's Love; Guidance; Homosexuality; "Just One More"; Marriage; Motives; OCD; Pornography; Pre-Engagement; Priorities; Procrastination; Self-Injury; Sexual Sin; Stress; Suffering; Suicide; Teens and Sex; Thankfulness; Why Me?, Worry.*

FOR FURTHER INFORMATION

Speaking engagements with our authors may be requested by visiting The Christian Counseling and Educational Foundation website: www.ccef.org Videotapes, DVDs, CDs and audio cassettes by our authors may be ordered through www.ccef.org